HENRIK LARSSON
A Season in Paradise

HENRIK LARSSON

A Season in Paradise

with Mark Sylvester

Published by BBC Worldwide Limited,
Woodlands, 80 Wood Lane, London W12 0TT

First published 2001
Copyright © Mark Sylvester 2001
The moral right of the author has been asserted.

ISBN 0 563 53427 3

Commisioning Editor: Ben Dunn
Project Editor: Helena Caldon
Copy-editor: Tim Glynne-Jones
Picture Researcher: Bea Thomas

Set in Sabon and Helvetica
Printed and bound in Great Britain by Butler & Tanner Ltd,
Frome and London
Colour separations by Radstock Reproductions Ltd, Midsomer Norton
Jacket printed by Lawrence-Allen, Weston-super-Mare

For further information about Henrik Larsson, go to his website at:
www.icons.com

ICONS.com

contents

one **escape** 9

two **the leg** 25

three **the big kick-off** 43

four **into europe** 59

five **the old firm** 71

six **the big disappointment** 83

seven **into winter** 95

eight **the break** 109

nine **welcome back** 121

ten **cup winners** 133

eleven **the treble** 147

twelve **sweden** 161

thirteen **paradise regained** 173

celtic results 185

index 189

picture credits 192

To everyone who made this treble-winning season possible

chapter one
escape

'Ladies and gentlemen, we'll soon be starting our descent into
Glasgow, so could you please make sure that your arm-rest is
down, your tray is stowed away and that your seat is in the upright
position.' I glanced around, but the stewardess' announcement
didn't seem to have any effect on my fellow passengers, other than a
slight rustling of papers being put away and rubbish being cleared.
There was a man across the aisle reading a newspaper, who looked
like he was on business, and just behind him a well-dressed woman
who kept peering nervously out of the window. Me? I had a big
smile on my face. To me Glasgow was like the promised land, the
place that was going to save me, and my career. I was escaping.

I folded away the tray in front of me and thought of a movie
I'd seen, in which some British prisoners of war had spent months
planning an escape from a German prison camp. They sweated over
digging a tunnel, hid the soil and then, just as they were about to
make their break, they were caught and thrown into solitary con-
finement. When they were released from solitary, they tried again
and this time they got away. They spent days on the run, hiding out
in barns, sneaking on to the goods wagons of trains, stealing bicycles,
climbing mountains, desperately trying to put as much distance

between themselves and the prison camp as possible. One night, the
only place they could find to sleep was behind some bushes. In the
morning, they woke up and there was a soldier standing over them
with a gun. You could see their faces fall. After all they had been
through, to fail now seemed so cruel. And then the soldier spoke
and it turned out he was Swiss. They had spent the last day in
Switzerland. They laughed and threw their arms around each other,
and then threw their arms around the slightly bewildered soldier.
They couldn't believe they'd escaped.

It might sound slightly dramatic, but the way those guys felt at
that moment is a little bit like how I was feeling on that flight. I was
escaping from a nightmare in Rotterdam and I couldn't be sure
that I wouldn't be throwing my arms around the customs officer
in the airport terminal. I could see the date on the businessman's
newspaper: 28 July 1997. It was a date I was going to remember –
the day I signed for Celtic.

The flight from Amsterdam's Schipol airport to Glasgow takes
only a couple of hours, but I was sure that it was a journey that
was going to change my life. I was too excited to eat and I couldn't
concentrate on reading anything, so I ended up staring at the
passing clouds with my nose almost pressed against the window,
running over in my mind all the things that had happened in the last
couple of months, all the things that had brought me to this point.

As I sat there, with my ears starting to feel the pressure of our
descent, I was still a professional footballer signed to Feyenoord
Football Club of Rotterdam, Holland. But I had become easily the
most miserable professional footballer in Rotterdam, if not the
whole of Holland. In fact, to say I was playing football for Feyenoord

would have been an overstatement. Yes, I was a Feyenoord player, but I was rarely getting a chance to play. The coach obviously didn't rate me and now I was desperate to leave.

Outside the aeroplane window I could see that we were just breaking through the bottom of the clouds. Below us small lakes nestled between rugged hills, shining in the early afternoon sun. It looked beautiful, just like the promised land should look. And, I have to say, the sun was a welcome surprise. The players back at Feyenoord had said goodbye, and wished me luck, and then warned me about the Scottish weather. 'It rains all the time,' they said. 'Better take your scuba gear with you.' Well, I looked forward to telling them they were wrong. They were a good bunch and I would miss them, but good teammates and a few decent restaurants were the only thing I was going to miss.

I took a sip of water and tried to remember exactly how it had all gone so wrong at Feyenoord. It certainly was a far cry from how I'd felt when I joined the club from Helsingborgs IF, my first professional side, in my native Sweden. Then it had been a huge adventure – a new country, a new lifestyle and a chance to prove myself with one of the big names of European football. When I signed, I wanted to shout, 'This is it, I've made it!' I had been flattered that a club like Feyenoord wanted me. I was 22 and I knew it was the right time to make a move. I had achieved a lot at home in Sweden and now I needed a new challenge abroad. I looked forward to pitting myself against new players and some of the world's best defenders.

There had been times during the early part of my career in Sweden when I didn't even think I was going to make it as a professional footballer at all. I'm sure plenty of pro's have doubts, but I had been dogged by them. In fact, when I was only 13, I seriously thought about giving up football completely. As a kid I was always being told that I had talent. I certainly seemed to have an instinct for scoring goals, but, by the time I reached my teens, my progress towards footballing glory appeared to have come up against a pretty tough obstacle – my size. While the other lads were rocketing up all around me into big, strong men, I remained small and decidedly lightweight.

I spent more time as a sub watching my friends play than I did playing myself. I was on the point of quitting when Bengt Perssön, the coach of Hogaborg BK, my home town's under-15 side, grabbed me after another awful game in which I'd hardly touched the ball. I suppose it would have been easy for him not to bother with me – he could have just let me drift off, lose interest in football and end up in some completely different walk of life – but he didn't.

That day after our match, instead of going off home for his dinner, Bengt had decided to spend a few minutes with me. He obviously saw something in me that I didn't see myself, and for that I'll always be grateful. I reckon I must have looked like a big baby to Bengt, sulking away because I wasn't winning the ball and the big boys were knocking me around. I also wasn't very good at taking advice and, when he called me over, I shuffled towards him, wishing he would just let me get away.

'Henrik, what are you worrying about?' he said. 'You have a lot of ability in those feet and you know how to play football up here.' He pointed to his head. 'What you have to do is believe both those things. You will grow, it might just take a bit longer, and if you train hard you'll be strong like the other boys. Now go off home and stop feeling sorry for yourself.'

Of course, he was right. Over the years I've realized that if you have talent you will get on, but you also have to work hard and be dedicated. If I play well, to the best of my ability, and I lose, I can go to sleep that night. But if I let the team down because I didn't train properly, my fitness wasn't what it should have been and so I couldn't reach a ball, I wouldn't be able to sleep. I would not be able to look my teammates in the eye, and I certainly couldn't face the fans. You see again and again that the best teams are the ones whose players are not only skilful but are also prepared to work hard.

From the plane now I could see a small golf course. I had started to really get into the game and I thought about playing a few rounds at Scotland's famous clubs on my days off. Then there were houses, laid out in crescents, with tall apartment blocks in between and concrete squares with kids running about chasing footballs. This was Glasgow and, if everything went well, it was going to be my new home. And that, inevitably, led me back to thinking about my arrival in Rotterdam.

I suppose the one thing I had really wanted when I left Helsingborgs was to make people back home proud of me. Sweden has some good football teams and some great players, but there are still not many professional sides, and relatively few Swedes play abroad. When you leave the country many people in Sweden follow your progress really closely. They want you to do well. It's as if you are an ambassador for the country and its league. I was determined that I would live up to their expectations and become a success abroad. I always knew I would go back to Sweden at some point and I didn't want to go back with my tail between my legs. I wanted to go back having achieved something. To begin with, it looked like those dreams would come true at Feyenoord.

I had actually come close to joining Grasshoppers of Zurich, since they were the first foreign club to make Helsingborgs a decent offer. But, with all due respect to the Swiss team, as soon as I discovered Feyenoord had come in for me, there really wasn't a lot of competition. Apparently they had been watching me for a while and were obviously impressed with the 50 goals that I'd managed to score in two seasons, the first of which had seen Helsingborgs' promotion to the Swedish Premier League for the first time in 22 years.

Feyenoord paid £295,000 for me, which is peanuts by today's standards, and even in 1993 was not a lot of money. But half of that fee went to my first club, Hogaborg, and it was really nice to help out a little team in my home town. The team director at Feyenoord was Wim Jansen, who was a very respected coach, and would play an important part in my career. I think if he had not later left the club, things might have been very different. Once my wife, Magdalena, arrived we settled into a nice life, learned to speak Dutch, got to know the good places to eat and made some nice friends. I struck up a great friendship with Orlando Trustfull, one of my new teammates, and we played a bit of pool and snooker together. Then Magdalena became friends with Orlando's wife and the four of us would see a lot of each other. This was very important to me. I'm not the sort of person who is happy to just play football and train, I like having a good home life and a way of escaping from the pressure that professional footballers come under all the time.

I was playing quite well in that first season and, although I only scored one goal in 16 games, I had worked hard and was breaking into the Swedish national team. The following season, I took my goal tally to 11, and that summer I went with the Swedish squad to the World Cup in America. I spent a lot of time on the bench, but came on as a sub against Cameroon, played the whole game against Brazil and scored from the spot in our penalty shoot-out with Romania in the quarter-final. We were soundly beaten by Brazil in the semi-final, another game in which I helped keep the bench warm, but we won the third/fourth place play-off 4–1 against Bulgaria, and I scored.

Ask any player what his ambitions were when he first started his career and I'm sure most would list scoring in the World Cup Finals as one of them. It's certainly a memory that has stayed with me and is as clear today as it was seconds after it had happened. I was just inside the Bulgarian half when Kennet Anderson played a square ball to me and I was able to push it past a defender. I closed in on the keeper and, as he came out, I got it past him too. He was on the floor and suddenly the goal was there, right in front of me. In moments like that your mind is racing, selecting the right thing to do, like a fighter pilot deciding what weapon to use next. Before I could shoot, another defender came flying across to block the attempt. I dummied to shoot with my left and he went sprawling. I rounded him and rolled the ball over the line. What a feeling that was! My football seemed as though it was going in exactly the right direction. The following season at Feyenoord went quite well and we reached the semi-finals of the European Cup, losing to Real Zaragoza. But by the 1995–96 season, there were storm clouds on the horizon.

Wim Jansen, my friend, coach and, to some extent, my mentor, left the club, and with that my career at Feyenoord started to unravel, along with my life in Rotterdam. The new coach, Arie Haan, had different ideas about how he wanted the team to play, and certainly had different ideas about what he wanted from me. I'd like to think that I'm a good team player. I know that no player is bigger than the club he plays for and I know that the coach's first priority is to that club. I'm not saying that I would ever be happy about being dropped or substituted, but I know that there are going to be times when it is the right thing to do, and I accept that. But at Feyenoord, I soon started to believe that the coach was wrong and that what he was doing was not good for the team.

One week I would be playing on the right wing, the next I'd be switched to the left. Then I'd be moved into midfield. And, as well as being switched all around the park, I was being substituted in every game that I started. I know what I'm capable of and the simple fact is that I wasn't being given a chance to do it. My confidence was being affected, my game started suffering and it wasn't long before I knew that my performance was falling well below the standard that I expected of myself.

Some of the newspapers were starting to get on my back and at first all I had in mind was to prove them wrong. I'm no quitter. Right from my earliest days playing football with all the neighbourhood kids in a field at the bottom of our garden, I had wanted to win. But as the weeks of frustration at Feyenoord turned to months, I began to wish I could get away. Some people might think I was wrong to react in that way, but I would argue that it's really difficult to motivate yourself and play well when you know you're going to be taken off after 60 minutes. I wanted to be in a position where I could have some say in how and where I played, but it seemed I just wasn't going to be given that chance. The coach was choosing players ahead of me, some of whom who I didn't even think should be at the club.

Before long, my unhappiness at the club began to affect the rest of my life. I became quite moody and difficult to live with. I talked a lot with Magdalena and we tried to work out what was best for us. We had travelled to a new country so that I could pursue my football career and so that we could experience a new life, but now things were going badly wrong. She had been with me during the good times in Sweden and had supported me when I said we should move to Holland. It can be tough for a footballer's wife, because you know there is always a chance you might have to move, no matter how much you like a place, no matter how close you are to the people there. The career comes first and it can be very unsettling.

Magdalena is an amazing woman. She has never complained about the life. I suppose she chose me when I was a footballer and accepted all the things that go with it, the good and the bad. After seven years together, she knew me almost better than I knew myself, and talking with her helped me get things straight in my mind. Our life was suffering and that had to stop for both our sakes. We hadn't come to Holland to be unhappy. You can only keep going for so long in a situation like that. At first you think that, if you keep battling and doing your best, things will change. But there does come a time when you realize that there is nothing more you can do, that you are just hitting your head against a brick wall.

To say I was unhappy would be playing it down a lot. By May, the last month of the 1996–97 season, I had made up my mind. I was going to leave and I wanted to get away as fast as possible. I just thought to myself, I've done everything I can, it isn't working, I've got to leave. And fortunately there was a way.

When I'd joined Feyenoord, I'd had a clause written into my contract stating that if a club came in with an offer of £600,000 or more, and I wanted to go, I could. Of course, the tough thing then is finding another club that wants you. I rang my agent and told him to get me out of there. I told him to ask around and see if anybody was interested in me. Soon afterwards I gave an interview to a Swedish newspaper saying that I wanted to leave Feyenoord and explaining my reasons, and it wasn't long before that news made its way back to the club and things turned from bad to worse.

I'm sure it's tough for anyone if they are doing a job that they don't enjoy, working for a boss they don't get on with in an office or a factory they have grown to hate, and where they are not appreciated. It's the same for a footballer. You begin to hate the moment the alarm goes off in the morning, the drive to work. There were times at Feyenoord when I would just lie in bed hoping the phone would ring and my agent would tell me this great club or that great club wanted me. I simply dreaded going into the club, especially on match days when I knew I would spend most, if not all, of the game with my tracksuit on. I even started to hate that tracksuit. If you are not a regular in the first team, it is easy to start feeling that you aren't really part of the club, that you don't figure in its plans. The other players were still great, I knew they rated me and could see what was happening, but there was nothing anyone could have done. My fate at Feyenoord seemed sealed.

The most important thing at a time like that is not to forget that you do have ability. The lesson on that cold afternoon from Bengt Perssön had stuck, and enough had happened to me since to give me faith in my ability. Whenever I was given the chance, I had always scored goals and I'd even scored in the World Cup Finals. Still, I was struggling to retain my confidence and, if I had had to stay much longer in Rotterdam, I can't say what might have happened to me.

I was so desperate to leave that I contacted my old club, Helsingborgs IF, and basically told them that I might be available if they were interested in making the crucial £600,000 offer. Representatives of Helsingborgs came to Holland and we sat down and talked. I made it clear that I was quite happy to go home and to start all over again but that, at the same time, my agent was still looking around and, if another decent offer came in, I might take it. They understood completely. I love Sweden and there would not have been a real hardship in going back, but I had only been away for three and a half years, and I really didn't feel I had achieved anywhere near the level of success that I wanted abroad.

Then it happened. I was sitting at home thinking about moving back to Sweden, when the phone rang. It was my agent Rob Jansen. For some reason, as soon as I picked up the phone I felt it was going to be good news. 'So, Henrik, what do you think about Celtic?' I felt my heart skip a beat. 'They're very interested in you and want to meet you in my office tomorrow. Can you make it?' Could I make it! Try stopping me. Rob laughed. He knew this was a great opportunity and I could hear the excitement in his voice.

Rob is more than an agent to me, he's also a friend, who I know is always looking out for me and who I trust totally. I think he'd also probably got a little tired of me calling him to tell him to get me out. Agents come in for a lot of criticism, but many of them do a great job and have the best interests of the players at heart. These days footballers are so busy, with the number of games they have to play and the level of training required, that it's impossible for them to manage their own affairs. I told Rob that I'd be in at whatever time he wanted me. I would have jumped in my car there and then if it could have made things happen any quicker. I put the phone down and turned to Magdalena, who was holding her breath. She could tell something interesting was about to happen. 'We don't have to go back to Sweden just yet,' I smiled. 'It's Celtic.' She smiled back, and said, 'I'm not moving without my dog' before throwing her arms around me.'

To say I was excited would be an understatement. It was a bit like the time Feyenoord came in when I was about to join Grasshoppers – the rabbit had been pulled from the hat at the last moment. The magic ingredient was Wim Jansen, who was taking over as coach at Celtic and had obviously heard about my predicament. Most importantly, he was prepared to offer Feyenoord the crucial £600,000 that would unlock my contract. There wasn't a moment's hesitation on my part. I knew a bit about Celtic. I knew they were a big club with a rich history and I had learned all about their defeat to Feyenoord in the 1970 European Cup Final. On top of that, of course, I knew Wim Jansen very well and I was pretty sure that he wouldn't have taken the job at Celtic if he hadn't been confident that it was a club that was going places. In fact, I have so much respect for him that, even if I had known nothing about Celtic at all, his word would have been good enough. The funny thing was that I didn't speak to him at all at that stage. I didn't need to. All I needed to know was that Celtic had offered me a lifeline.

Because of the contract, I didn't feel any need to talk to Feyenoord about what I was doing. It was plain that I could go for the right money, so I set about the usual tasks you have to complete before signing for a club. I had to get all my details from Feyenoord to take to Celtic for my medical examination, and I suppose it became the worst kept secret in Rotterdam that I was in talks with the Scottish giants. The fact that I didn't approach Arie Haan really shouldn't have been a problem. I was well within my rights to talk to Celtic and it was clear that Feyenoord didn't have any use for me. I figured I could sort out my move and everybody would be happy. So I was stunned when I returned from my Celtic medical to find that Feyenoord were contesting the move.

I couldn't believe I was going to have to fight a court case before I would be able to escape. I was really angry. Not only were they making my life hell but, now that I had a chance to get away and start to rebuild my career, they were putting obstacles in my way. I was sure that I would win the case, but it seemed malicious and petty. I don't think Feyenoord were interested in keeping me, but I suppose they were sure they could get more than £600,000, and they wanted to hold on to me until a better offer came in. The thought of hanging around while they looked at offers made me feel sick. The more I thought about Celtic, the more I knew it was exactly the right place for me to go.

The case was to be heard at the headquarters of the Dutch Football Association at Zeist. And, although it was more of a tribunal than an actual law court, it was all very formal. I had to turn up in a suit and answer questions. There were representatives of Feyenoord, and there was Rob. It was an odd feeling to sit there in a sports court like a criminal on trial, when all I wanted to do was play football and fulfil the terms of my contract. I was sure I had right on my side, but there is always a nagging doubt in the back of your mind, that some horrible injustice will take place. From the first moment your best friend breaks a window with a football and blames you, all boys expect bad things to happen with authority.

The two weeks between the end of the case and the verdict were two of the worst I have ever experienced. We were in pre-season training and the team was spending the mornings running and working on fitness, then playing games in the afternoon. I had to train, but in the afternoon the coach wouldn't let me play. I had to get changed and just sit there on the bench watching my teammates having a mini match. One day I decided I'd had enough of being treated that way. I turned to the coach and, with real frustration in my voice, said, 'I just don't understand you. Why don't you just let me go, since you obviously don't have any use for me here? I want to play football, but you don't appreciate me at all.' He told me that he had said to the club that he was happy for me to leave, but the president didn't want me to go. Perhaps the president quite liked me. Or, more likely, I know there were people at the club who believed in me. Of course, I'm sure they didn't want me to go for a mere £600,000.

A few days later, I was sitting in front of the hotel TV at the training camp, and I idly flicked the channel over to Teletext. Just for a second, I couldn't believe my eyes and I felt my heart pounding in my chest. There it was, clear as anything, my name and a bunch of other words that were practically swimming before me: 'TRIBUNAL SAYS LARSSON CAN GO.' I felt a huge weight lift off my shoulders. Free at last, I thought. Free at last. I didn't want to waste another second. I went straight to see the other players and say goodbye, because I didn't intend setting foot inside Feyenoord ever again. The players were really good about it, because they knew what I was going through. We used to get a little allowance for expenses when we were at the training camp, around 600 guilders, which is about £180, so I gave mine to the boys and told them to go and have a few drinks on me and have a good night. I shook them all by the hand and that was it, I was gone.

Of course, it was another big move and there were lots of things to think about. Wim Jansen had told me the Scottish people were great, really friendly and good fun. We also had to find a home for our dog, a huge Rhodesian Ridgeback. Leaving our friends and the dog were our biggest regrets. The plan was for me to go over first and get all the official stuff sorted out, then Magdalena would follow and we'd find somewhere to live. I suddenly felt alive again. The months of moping were behind me, and I had a new life and a new challenge ahead. The plane's wheels hit the runway with a thud and I thought again of those soldiers in the film. 'Ladies and gentlemen, welcome to Glasgow.' That smile was back on my face, and in my head I said, 'Thanks.' Now, where were those customs officers?

chapter two
the leg

There are some moments in life when everything just stops, when the traffic stops roaring, or the birds stop singing and even your heart seems to come to a grinding halt. It happens when someone gives you bad news, or you see something awful. For me it happened at 7.42 pm on Tuesday, 21 October 1999, the moment that my tibia snapped in half.

It's still quite difficult for me to talk about that horror, because it is something both I and my family have tried really hard to put behind us. I've never liked dwelling on bad things and I prefer to keep looking forward, taking each new challenge as it comes. But breaking my leg like that is not something I can forget and there are enough photos of the incident all over the place to keep reminding me. If I am honest with myself, I know it is always somewhere in the back of my mind, but it does make me more grateful for all the good things that have happened to me since.

More than the injury itself, I suppose what really got me down was the time I lost when I could have been helping Celtic to win something. I'm not so big-headed as to think that I would have made a huge difference to the season, but at the time I was injured we were really starting to put some good performances together.

We had high hopes when we travelled to Lyon for that UEFA Cup match against Olympique. We had every right to be confident. I had scored seven goals in seven games and the team was starting to show real belief in itself.

Since joining Celtic, my career had really got back on course and I was loving my time in Scotland in every way, even though I'd had something of a disastrous start. During my first game in a Celtic shirt, against Hibs, I had given the ball away just outside our penalty area and they had scored. We lost 2–1 and, as I sat in the dressing room afterwards, I knew it was time for a moment of honesty. 'Look, boys, we lost that game because I gave the ball away. It was my fault.' It was then that I first heard an expression that was going to become pretty familiar. 'Nae bother.' I wasn't totally sure what it meant at the time, but I could tell they appreciated that I wasn't trying to duck responsibility. Obviously, I was less than pleased to have messed up my first outing for the 'Bhoys', but it made me determined to put things right and the season soon started to get better.

By the time the final whistle of the season went in the game against St Johnstone in May, I had scored 16 goals and, much more importantly, Celtic had won the league. It was their first champion-ship in nine years and it prevented Rangers from beating the Celtic record of nine in a row. It had not taken me long to understand the significance of that. The importance of the rivalry between the Old Firm is immediately apparent to any foreigner in Glasgow, and, even as a Swede, I soon got caught up in the passion of the contest. We felt great handing the championship to our fans, and sparing them another summer of taunts.

The following year, 1998–99, had not been so good. Although personally I'd had one of my best seasons ever, I would have traded any individual achievement for one bit of silverware for the club. I managed to get on the score sheet 39 times, including 29 in the league, and was voted Players' Player of the Year and Football Writers' Player of the Year. My dreams of being successful abroad were really coming true now. But, of course, we lost our title and were beaten in the final of the Scottish Cup.

That is why the 1999–2000 season was so important. We knew we had a good team, possibly as good as the one that had won the championship in 1998, and we were determined to repeat that triumph. The last thing you want is for people to start saying, 'Oh, it was just a one-off. They're just a flash in the pan.' We knew that wasn't the case, that there was more to us than a one-season wonder.

As well as our domestic ambitions, though, we were keen to do well in the UEFA Cup. It's always tough playing away in a European tie. You want to keep things tight, not give too much away but also try to grab a valuable away goal that will force the opposition into doing something reckless. European football can be a bit of a chess match at times, and that is how the game against Lyon was going.

As much as I might want to forget them, the seconds that led up to my injury are there, engraved on my brain. It's like a DVD that I can replay in my head any time I choose (of course, most of the time I keep it on stop). I remember clearly that Olympique had possession out on the right and I could see that the player on the ball was going to swing it over to the left, to a guy who was a few yards in front of me. My first thought was to close him down and I knew it was important to time my run exactly right, so that I would arrive there just at the same time as the ball. I knew that he would try to pull it down, and in those few seconds before he had brought it under control I would have the chance to nick it away.

In my DVD version of what happened next, everything is in slow-motion. The sound of the crowd becomes this low hum and the ball seems to take for ever to fly through the air. I had it clear in my mind exactly what I was going to do. I would plant my left leg firmly on the ground and make the tackle with my right. But, as my left foot hit the ground, my studs seemed to jam in the turf while my weight was still going forward. There was a crack, which seemed to me to be louder than all the voices of the crowd, and at this point my DVD switches to pause.

I don't know exactly how I fell, because the next thing I remember was being flat on my back, thinking, 'Something's not right here.' For some reason I kept my left leg up in the air, so when I raised my head I could see it above me, with the bottom part hanging down. Although I could plainly see that it was very bad, there was no sense of panic. Strangely, it didn't really hurt either and I think that is because I had gone into shock. Although everything seemed to have stopped around me, my mind was moving fast, thinking rationally. It's probably like the person who has been told they've been given the sack. While they are stunned, at the same time they're thinking, 'okay, how do I go about getting another job?'

I called over to the ref, who was Dutch, to stop the game and to get me some help. Then I brought my leg gently down, because it was too much of an effort to keep it in the air. By this time people were crowding around me and I knew they were saying things to me, but I wasn't really listening. There was just movement and noise. I was thinking about Magdalena and hoping she hadn't seen it on TV. I wanted to be able to call her as soon as possible, to reassure her that everything was okay.

By now I'd put my leg back down because it was starting to ache, and I could see that it was at some weird angle on the ground. Medics had rushed on to the pitch and, before they loaded me on to the stretcher, they put my leg in place because they were worried that the bone would pierce the skin, and that could cause all sorts of problems with infection. Within a few minutes, I was being carried to the dressing room. I have a vague memory of faces staring down at me, but all I was thinking about was getting to that phone and speaking to Magdalena. There was a little, well-equipped medical room in the ground and, once I had been brought into there, someone passed me my mobile. Whatever people may say about mobile phones, this was one occasion when I gave thanks that they had been invented.

When the home phone was picked up, I spoke in Swedish. 'Hi, Magdalena, it's me. You saw it on TV, right? It's okay, I'm fine. The people here are looking after me and I'm pretty sure everything's going to be all right.' Magdalena was trying to sound calm, but I could tell that she was really worried. She is very strong, but I'm sure the TV pictures had made what happened look terrible. You wonder sometimes whether the people who show something like that over and over again ever stop to think of the family of the injured person.

I wanted to be able to speak to Magdalena for longer, to keep telling her it was going to be all right, but the paramedics wanted to give me painkillers and get me ready for the journey to the hospital. I made one more phone call, to my mother in Sweden, because I knew it wouldn't be long before my parents found out what had happened and I wanted them to hear it from me first. My parents were terrified and I think their first fear was that it was the end of my career. In some ways it's probably worse when something like this happens to somebody you love than if it actually happens to you. I was being told exactly what was going on and being constantly reassured. My parents were hundreds of miles away, worrying.

The funny thing is that I didn't for one moment imagine this was going to be it, that I would not recover. Even lying there in the ambulance, having seen my leg hanging in half, I wasn't making plans for what I would do if I had to pack it in. Which is lucky, because I still have no idea what I would do outside of football. I don't know if this is common with players who suffer a bad injury, but I felt sure I would be back. What I was thinking was how quickly I could make it. I wanted to be able to run out on a pitch again. Right away I decided that I would get fit again and then see how good I was going to be.

In the stadium's medical room they had given me a shot of morphine to numb the pain, which they seemed sure would kick in soon, so by the time I reached the hospital I was feeling a bit wasted. The staff at the hospital were tremendous. There wasn't a specialist on duty at the time, but they sent for him and then began to examine the injury. The worry then, apparently, was that there might be further injury and so they took a series of X-rays to investigate what had happened when my leg broke. Even though I was drugged on morphine, I understood what was going on and I waited anxiously to hear what the doctors had to say.

Quite often, it is the other problems around a leg break that can cause complications. A clean break will normally mend and, with modern surgery, can be as strong as it was before. But, when a bone breaks, it can pull tendons out of place, tear muscle and make a real mess. You could say I was a bit relieved when the X-rays came back and they showed there was no other damage. They put my leg in plaster and I was driven to the airport to catch the same shuttle flight back to Glasgow that my teammates would be on.

I arrived first and they loaded me on to the front of the plane. Of course, that meant every single person who got on after me had to walk past. Most of them wanted to talk to me, but didn't really know what to say. And it wasn't just the players. All the Celtic officials and journalists were on the flight as well, so I had a succession of people filing past, asking if I was okay and staring at the ground. I remember almost nothing of the flight home.

My leg was really starting to hurt despite the morphine, which was making everything seem very strange. It seemed weird how a split second can change everything. In my slightly fevered state I started thinking how a touch I'd had earlier in the game had led to my breaking a leg. If one thing had been different before, if I hadn't made the run exactly when I did, or if the guy had hesitated in making the pass, I'd now be sitting next to Marc Rieper discussing golf swings, not facing a long fight back to fitness.

The rest of the night is a blur. From the plane, I was taken to Southern General Hospital, where I slept badly through the night.

When I woke up, Magdalena was there with our little boy Jordan, who was only two-and-a-half and had no idea why his dad wasn't at home. He'd been born the month before I moved to Glasgow, which had obviously been a pretty hectic period in our life. We'd named him after the great basketball player, Michael Jordan, and he had become the centre of our universe. He was growing up with a bit of a Scots accent, which was fine, but it was becoming a battle to get him to speak Swedish. We were determined that he should grow up knowing both English – with a Glasgow accent – and Swedish. But our plan wasn't going that well. 'I don't want to speak Swedish, daddy,' he'd say. I tried there in the hospital, but he wasn't having any of it.

Magdalena was trying not to appear upset. It was pretty tough for her to see me like that and she was putting on a brave face, both for me and for Jordan. While we were talking, the surgeon who was going to perform the operation arrived. He seemed very efficient, which I was glad to see, and talked positively about what was going to happen, but I suppose that's his job. Basically they were going to put a long metal pin in my leg to help the bones knit together. He said the X-ray showed it was a very clean break and there shouldn't be any complications. By now my leg was throbbing and seemed to be really hot. I wanted the operation to happen as soon as possible, because only then would I be able to start the fight back.

I'm not a huge fan of hospitals, to be honest. They really make me nervous. Luckily I'd never had to spend much time in one before that day. There is something about the smell, all that disinfectant, that simply gets to me. So I was glad when they told me that if the operation went well, I would be sent home soon afterwards. Before I was taken down for surgery I was given drugs to relax me and I was soon feeling pretty light-headed, not worrying one bit about what was going to happen, even though some of the lads had been going on about having to have my leg sawn off. I was wheeled down to the operating theatre and I remember watching the lights above my head as we went down corridors and turned corners. Once inside the theatre, they put a mask over my nose and mouth, and told me to count backwards from 10. I think I started in English, changed to Swedish and then I fell asleep.

The next thing I remember was waking up back in the hospital bed. As I slowly came round my heart suddenly skipped. Had it been successful? Had there been any complications? Did they think my leg would heal properly? The doctor came to see me and I could have hugged him when he told me everything had gone to plan. For some reason, after I woke up, I desperately wanted the toilet. I hadn't had much to drink for a long time, but the need to go was becoming unbearable. The nurses were anxious that I shouldn't try to get up, so they gave me a bed pan and left me to get on with it. But, try as I might, I just couldn't go in that thing, I seemed to have some kind of mental block about it, which was madness considering how badly I wanted to go. At that moment, I would have traded almost anything in order to go. I begged the nurses to put a catheter in, but they said it would be too painful. 'I've just got to go!' I shouted. 'You've got to do something.' They were obviously worried that I was going to scream the hospital down, so they relented and helped me to the toilet. The feeling of relief was overwhelming.

When Magdalena arrived with Jordan, I was lying in bed with an oxygen mask over my nose and mouth. 'I think you have to do

something about your image, Henrik,' she joked, although I think
she was a bit shocked to see me rigged up like that. Because there
were no complications, the hospital let me go home almost right
away and it was great to get back to our house in Bothwell.

In the end, finding a place to live had been quite easy. When
I first signed for Celtic I was travelling back and forth between
Scotland and Holland and mostly staying in an hotel in East
Kilbride. A few other players, like Reggie Blinker and Marc Rieper,
had just joined and were staying at the same hotel. I vaguely knew
Reggie from Holland, and the whole bunch of us got on really well.
We played a bit of pool and cards; it was as I imagine a boarding
school might be.

Of course, after a while you start to get tired of that sort of
life – professional footballers spend a lot of time on the road and
most of us now stay in an hotel before every game, home or away.
So Magdalena and I decided we would find a house. She flew over
one weekend and went off house hunting with the help of the
coach's wife, Cobe. After the second day she came back and said,
'I've seen somewhere I like and it's the nicest place I've seen,' and
that was it. I trusted her that it would be right and I didn't set foot
inside the place until we had workmen there putting in wooden
floors. Coming from Sweden, wooden floors are the thing and we
had to get rid of those carpets.

Apart from the fact that it's a nice house in a lovely area, it's just
a 15-minute drive from Celtic Park. I've never been somebody who
can cope with an hour's drive to train for a few hours, only to have
another hour's drive home. That would drive me crazy. So we made
our home in Bothwell and quickly settled in. I actually think it was

easy to adapt because Scotland is quite like Sweden. The country-side is similar and the people are just as warm.

Within a few days of getting out of hospital, I couldn't open the door in the mornings for all the Get Well cards. I was amazed at the response I got, and not only from Celtic fans. There were cards from all over Europe and, incredibly, quite a few from Rangers fans. I suppose when something like that happens, you realize that a lot of people are just football fans, pure and simple. They might want another team to win, but they don't like to see a player badly injured. Of course, the cards and letters from the Celtic fans meant most to me and made me more determined than ever to get fit and playing again.

Having said that, I had to remember what I had been through. I couldn't walk and, whenever I wanted to go anywhere, it was like a military operation on crutches. I spent most of my time lying on the sofa, catching up on a bit of reading and making myself a nuisance to Magdalena. Then, after a couple of days like that, it was time to go into Celtic to see the club doctor and physio, and discuss what we were going to do next.

In the doctor's room we sat down to plan the strategy. 'So, Henrik, d'ya think we should just take things a bit slow then?' asked Brian Scott. 'Yeah, that would be good because I have no idea how to even walk at the moment.' They laughed. We would just take it one day at a time and not set any come-back targets. I felt relieved by that. I didn't want the pressure of a deadline and I was really grateful that they were prepared to put the time and effort into helping me regain my fitness.

The plan was pretty straightforward. It only takes a few days for muscles to start to deteriorate and the important thing is to set them

working again as soon as possible before wastage becomes a real
problem. The easiest way to do so is with bike work, and it wasn't
long before I was eating up the kilometres without going anywhere.
I would just put my head down and pump away until Brian stopped
me. I'm sure it helped that I had always kept myself really fit, I
would never avoid anything in training, and now all those runs
were paying off.

Brian was incredibly patient, always trying to push me a little
further each day. A couple of weeks into the recovery programme,
I was sitting in the gym having a rest when Brian came over. 'OK,
Henrik, let's see you have a bit of a walk with that crutch of yours.'
I'd been walking a bit using just the one crutch, so I duly obliged
and tottered across the floor towards him. 'That's great,' said Brian.
'Now, why don't you put the other crutch down as well.' This was a
bit worrying. I hadn't tried to walk unaided before. I was concerned
that my leg wouldn't be able to take the weight and I would fall
flat on my face. But Brian had obviously made up his mind, so I
carefully laid the crutch down and stood up straight. My leg felt
tight and weak. I put my right foot forward, then took the strain
as I lifted my left after it. I did it again and kept on going until I'd
walked across the gym. I may have been walking like a duck, but
I was walking. It was a good feeling and my confidence soared.

The first couple of months on the road to recovery were fine.
Although I was still walking like a duck most of the time, I could
see real progress. Every few days I would feel I had reached another
step on the ladder to being fully fit. Then, suddenly, I hit a brick
wall. After three months, all the major progress seems to have been
made and you're left trying to make those all-important minor

improvements that will get you back on to a football pitch. It's tough because you get to a point where you can't really tell if things are changing or not. The danger is that you get over anxious and rush something, and that sends you hurtling back down the ladder. So I just had to take everything slowly. Every day I would get up and make the short trip into the Park for hours of work and sweat. I would run and cycle and generally just keep on building up strength and fitness. Day after day, going through the routines that Brian gave me, I just kept one thing in mind: that one day I would again put a green and white shirt on and run out on to the pitch at Celtic Park.

It helped that I had tremendous backing from the club. Never for a moment did they lose faith in me, or put me under any pressure. After the hard times I had been through at Feyenoord, it was wonderful to be part of a club that really seemed to care about its players. During the winter break we went to a training camp in Portugal where I started to do some serious running, and when there were no reporters around I would kick the ball about a bit, hitting it with my left foot. I also got the chance to play some golf with Marc Rieper.

In March I got the chance to play at last for the reserves. It was a cold evening and rain was pouring out of a grey sky, but that didn't matter to me, I was back on a football pitch. I felt a bit rusty and the pace of the game seemed rather fast, but I managed to score and it felt like I'd never been away. A game against St Johnstone followed and I scored again. Then we played Hearts. The game was going fine, I was starting to get to grips with being back on a pitch and I had a few good touches, when suddenly a tackle came in and I felt a heavy thud against my left leg, exactly where I had broken it.

I tried to stand up, but the pain made me wince. My heart sank. I just couldn't believe it, after all I'd been through, the months of work. I limped off the pitch and the press guys were asking me how I was. 'Yeah, fine, I just need to get it checked out, it's no problem,' I told them. I may have sounded okay, but I felt sick. We got to the hospital and my heart was racing. 'Please don't let it be broken again.' Luckily it wasn't. There was no serious damage, but the leg was very sore. I had hoped to get in a few games before the end of the season to give myself a chance of being considered for the Swedish squad for Euro 2000, but now that dream seemed shattered. I was sure there was no chance and I felt nearly as depressed as when I had first broken my leg.

I was able to walk, but I was limping badly and the wound was sore. As soon as I walked through the front door, Magdalena knew there was something wrong. I threw myself onto the sofa and stared at the wall. You start running through your mind whether there was anything you could have done differently. Had I gone back too soon? Should I have kept out of tough challenges? The fact is that I knew, if I were given that time again, I would have done the same thing. I was desperate to play, to show I was fit enough for Sweden. Magdalena put her hand on my arm. 'What are you going to do, Henrik?' 'I don't know,' I said. Then I remembered that Marc Rieper was off to Portugal to commentate on a friendly between Denmark and Portugal, and to take in a little golf. 'I'm going to Portugal with Marc,' I said. Magdalena knew I was really down and that I needed to get away and forget about football for a few days, so it was settled.

We flew out shortly afterwards, and Rieps had a great time – Danish TV was paying for his travel and accommodation and

Henrik Larsson was buying his lunches. I decided to forget about the leg and about football, and just relax. We played golf on the Monday, Tuesday and even the Wednesday morning of the game. I had to adapt my swing a bit to protect the leg, but it was just what I needed. On the flight back I made up my mind I wasn't going to be beaten. I'd worked too hard and for too long to give up.

As soon as I was back in Scotland I started running, and before long there was no pain in my leg at all. I had one last throw of the dice to try to make the Swedish squad, but it was important to get a game under my belt for them to even consider asking me over to train. There was only one league game left, against Dundee United at home, and I desperately wanted to play. I hadn't had a great deal to do with Kenny Dalglish, but now I needed to convince him to let me play against Dundee United.

I asked for a meeting with him and he called me into his office. Whatever people say about Kenny, I didn't have any real problems with him. He never interfered much with the way I wanted to play, so that was okay as far as I was concerned. As I walked down the corridor I was conscious of the fact that I looked fit again. There was no limp. In fact, that is one of the strange things about the injury, because before I broke my leg I used to walk with a slight limp anyway. I'm not sure why, but somehow breaking my leg had cured it.

Dalglish was sitting behind his desk and asked me to take a seat. I wanted to sound confident, so I came straight out with it. 'It's like this, boss. I feel really good, training has been going well and I'd like to play against Dundee United.' He waited until he was sure I'd finished and then said in his quiet but firm voice, 'No, I don't think so, Henrik. We can't risk you getting a knock now that could mean you spend the whole summer trying to get fit again.'

I felt slightly annoyed and desperate. 'Honestly, boss, I do feel fine. Please give me this chance. I'm sure I'll be okay.' He looked at me for a few moments longer, then said, 'Right, let me think about it. I'll let you know tomorrow.' I jumped up, thanked him and walked out, knowing I still had to convince him, but at least I'd been given a chance.

The following day, Friday, I was incredibly nervous driving to the training ground at Barrowfield, a few minutes from the Park. I don't think I've ever been sharper in training. I was running after everything, tackling people, never standing still. I tried not to look at Dalglish, because I didn't want to know what he was thinking. By the end, I was pretty knackered and, as we were walking off, he called me over. 'Okay,' he said, 'I'll give you 25 minutes.' In the end, I played half an hour, had a few good touches and felt I'd done everything I could to let the Swedish coach Lars Lagerback know I was available.

It paid off. A few days later I got the call to go to Sweden to train with the national squad. There were just two places going and I was convinced that if I trained hard enough I could make one of them mine. We trained and played a few practice matches, and what I didn't realize was that the coaching staff were studying me very closely. In fact, I was the star of a little video they were producing. My every move was being recorded and then played back, slowed down and paused. They studied my movement to make sure there wasn't any inhibition and checked that my speed hadn't been affected.

We moved to a training camp in Denmark and played against a team in Copenhagen. Then, after the game, the coach pulled me aside with a very serious look on his face. My heart sank at the thought that he was going to tell me I hadn't made it. 'Henrik, we're just about to announce the squad and you know I told you right at the start that, if you could prove you were one of the best 22 players I have available, you'd be going.' He paused for what seemed like an eternity. 'Well, you're in.'

Suddenly it was all worthwhile: the endless hours on the bike, until the pools of sweat gathered on the floor. I knew it was down to all the people at Celtic who had worked with me and, of course, Brian Scott more than anyone. I couldn't tell anybody until the squad was formally announced, but I may have made a quiet phone call to Bothwell and heard a small scream of happiness at the other end.

chapter three
the big kick-off

The European Championship was disappointing for Sweden.
We didn't play to our potential and, unfortunately, competitions like
that don't give you any time to get into your stride. If you have a
poor start, you're desperately chasing the other sides in your group.

Yet the training had been going really well and the spirit in the
camp was good, fired by some pretty competitive games of billiards
in the team hotel. I was rooming with Jorgen Petterson, the Kaiser-
slautern forward, who is a great bloke and easy to get on with, and
everything about the hotel suited me down to the ground. But it
wasn't all plain sailing. I was told that, because of my lack of match
fitness, I wouldn't be in the starting line-up for the opening game
against Belgium. I was disappointed, but I understood Lars
Lagerback's arguments. He wanted to start with an experienced
and totally fit team.

We began really well against the joint hosts, forcing a number of
free-kicks and putting them under a lot of pressure. But they were
equipped with a very strong defence and right at the heart of it was
a player called Joos Valgaeren. Joos was a real pain – strong and
committed – the sort of pain that has become a pleasure, as he now
does the same sort of job at the heart of the Celtic defence.

Despite all the pressure, we just couldn't find a way through and it was very frustrating for me, sitting on the bench. I really wanted to get out there and try to help, as well as showing that I was fit enough to play. Having withstood our early pressure, Belgium started to get back into the game and, just before half-time, they scored. Worse was to come. Just after half-time, we conceded a second goal and the game looked beyond us.

However, within 10 minutes we had pegged one back. All of us at Celtic know what a threat Johan Mjallby can be when he is pushing up, and Belgium found out that night in Brussels. Their keeper was trying to deal with a back pass and he stood on the ball, allowing Johan to sneak in and score. It was the sort of opportunist goal you always have to be on the lookout for when you are playing up front.

I was sent on to try and get the equalizer, but I only managed a few touches and didn't have time to get into any sort of rhythm. Just before the end, Patrik Andersson was shown the red card, ruling him out of the next game, and on the final whistle we trudged off, knowing we had it all to do against Turkey in Eindhoven.

At least I knew I was fit. I had had no reaction from the leg, and coach Lagerback told me I would be playing against Turkey. He simply told me to go out and prove that I was fit enough, and I was determined not to let him down.

Our plan was to keep things tight and try to play the ball on the ground, but Turkey played an aerial game and we seemed to get caught up in it. Both sides were slugging it out without really getting anywhere and I was finding it hard to create any sort of goalscoring opportunity. And so it went on all game, finishing 0–0,

which left us with Italy to beat, and relying on Turkey to beat
Belgium.

We set off against Italy with all guns blazing and Johan had a
header cleared off the line. Just as it was with Belgium, though,
we went a goal down just before half-time. Italy had an even better
defence than Belgium, possibly the best in the world, but we were a
big, strong side and we thought we could wear them down in the
second half.

With about 75 minutes on the clock, Patrik Andersson put a
great ball through their defence for me to run onto. I only had the
keeper to beat and, as he went down, I dragged the ball round him
and scored. It was an amazing feeling. After having thought I
wouldn't even make it to the finals, to score a goal was a dream.

There wasn't time to enjoy it, though, because two minutes from
time we fell to the genius of Alessandro del Piero. He scored an
excellent goal and that was the end of our Euro 2000. We were all
disappointed because we hadn't played nearly as well as we had
done in qualifying, but for me there was some consolation. I was
named Man of the Match against Italy and I knew I could score
against the best defenders in the world. And to add to that, my leg
had come through unscathed.

The squad split up the day we were eliminated. That's the way it
is. Everybody was a little bit down and just wanted to get away to
their families. We took a short holiday to America and then I shot
back to Sweden to organize a stag night for my best friend. It was
nothing outrageous, nothing wild. I couldn't go crazy because Celtic
had started pre-season training and I had to get to Denmark in one
piece to meet up with them.

It was good to be back among the boys. I was excited because I knew I could still play football reasonably well after my injury. All the time I was fighting back, I never doubted I would get fit again, but the one thing that constantly nagged at the back of my mind was how well I'd be able to play. Until you get back out on the pitch, you just don't know how you might be affected. But, despite the disappointments of Euro 2000, I thought I'd played okay. I'd been up against some pretty good defenders and I'd scored quite a good goal.

Now there was a buzz in the Celtic camp, a real belief that we would do better than the previous season. You could feel that the players desperately wanted the season to get under way. This may have been the desire to put past disappointments behind us, but it also had something to do with the figure watching quietly from the sidelines. Kenny Dalglish had gone and Martin O'Neill had been lured away from Leicester City to be our new manager. It was a bit of a result, as we knew how highly thought of he was in the English Premiership. Obviously the lure of such a big club, with so much potential, was too much for him to resist.

He came over to watch us train in Denmark but kept fairly quiet. There wasn't any big speech about what he wanted to do or what he expected, he just stood back and watched, assessing what he had. He was looking at the players in the squad, deciding where he might need to bring people in and what our strengths and weaknesses were.

I didn't know a huge amount about Mr O'Neill at that point. I've watched a lot of English football, so I was aware of his achievements, and some of the other boys said they knew he liked

players who worked hard and would give their all for the club.
So obviously we were all putting in 110 per cent effort. No matter
what you might have done at a club, when a new coach turns up
you know you have to impress him and show him you deserve to
be in the side. My first impression of Mr O'Neill was that he
seemed very professional, quiet and thoughtful. It was a while
before he started making any significant changes, but right from
the start, he began to bring the best out of us.

Before the start of the season, and over the following weeks, he
would bring in a number of players to help strengthen the squad.
It's always good to get new blood into a club because it shows the
club is ambitious and the competition for places keeps players on
their toes. One of the early signings was Joos Valgaeren, the man
who had performed so well for Belgium in Sweden's opening Euro
2000 match. Obviously the new manager had been looking at him
during the championships as well, and it was no surprise that Joos's
performance had convinced Mr O'Neill to sign him up.

I think he was keen to bring in players who had different sides
to their game. Joos is very good in the tackle, but he can make
things happen in front of him as well. He is very strong and
competitive and a good guy to have around the club. And he was
obviously keen to come to Celtic, because he could have chosen
from a number of clubs, including several English ones. Footballers
know there is something special about Celtic and it can act as a
strong magnet.

Another player who was looking to make his debut in our first
game of the season, at Dundee United, was Chris Sutton. I knew a
bit more about Chris from the English football I'd watched and,

I'm sure Chris won't mind me saying this, he had been around for quite a while. I'd seen him at Norwich and then at Blackburn, where he played brilliantly alongside Alan Shearer and helped make Blackburn one of the top English sides. I knew that he was a big, strong player, who could hold the ball up well. He had nothing to prove when he came to Celtic, despite not having had a great time at Chelsea. Sometimes things just don't work out at a club, I know that as much as anyone. It doesn't mean there is anything wrong with you as a player, you just might not be right for that team, or that coach.

Alan Thompson was another key signing. Tommo gives the team a lot of options because he can play wide on the left, or in the middle, and there are not many people around with a left foot as strong as his. There was no lack of respect for the boys who were already here, but the manager knew that, if he wanted to change the way we played, he had to bring in some other players.

You hear stories about the nightmares that some players have at a new club, but I'm happy to say that isn't the case at Celtic. It really is a friendly club. It's right that the players should welcome new teammates and try to make them feel part of the club quickly. We have all moved around and know what that 'first day of school' feeling is like. You're a bit nervous, you might not know anybody and you're worried that somebody might think you are there to take their place. Some players immediately settle in, others need a bit more help.

At Celtic, new players are always met by our club captain, Tom Boyd. He takes them around the dressing room and introduces them to each player individually. I remember when I arrived going through that routine. Then it's up to you to train hard, show you are a team player and that you are worth being there.

The other important addition to the club was the new coach, Steve Walford. Obviously he was somebody the boss was very keen to bring in as soon as possible. They had been together for some time and knew each other very well. It's important for a new manager to build his team up with people he knows he can trust and who share his views on the way the game should be played. Even with a new manager and new coaching staff, things don't change immediately at a club. There is a slow change-over to new ways of doing things and different training regimes. Initially, in pre-season training, all you are concentrating on is getting fit again anyway. Most players keep themselves pretty fit over the summer, but if you are not playing football every week you inevitably lose a degree of sharpness. Of course, a few of us had been playing in Euro 2000, so we were probably better prepared than those who hadn't had that opportunity.

Stevie Walford didn't try to change everything from the start. There are certain things that you simply have to do in training – basic speed and fitness work, for instance, are common to all systems. But after a short while the way we were training did change, and I really liked it. We started to play a lot of games, with the defence against the attack and that sort of thing. I like there to be a point to what we are doing. Rather than just practising a dead ball situation, or knocking the ball around, piggy-in-the-middle style, I think it's better to have a proper purpose. You can stop games at any time and talk through a move, but it's still better to do it in the context of that game. Let's face it, football matches don't happen where one side does something, then the other gets a turn. You have to make it realistic. I soon started to really enjoy training and I think most of the other players did too. It was the perfect sort of preparation. You have to run to keep your stamina up, but I think we started to reach levels of fitness that we'd never had before, simply through training games where everybody was enjoying themselves and working very hard. I don't know if we started working harder under Stevie and Martin O'Neill, but I know players wanted to give their all.

Every coach has a vision of the way he wants his team to play and some coaches are better than others at communicating that to the players. I don't want to talk about previous managers at Celtic because every manager does his best, and does what he thinks is right. But I think all the players here would agree that Mr O'Neill expresses his vision of the way he wants us to play more clearly than any earlier manager ever did. The manager, Stevie and John Robertson are a great team and they have a way of putting ideas over to players that are easy to grasp.

It was quite funny when John Robertson was brought in. As a Swede I knew all about him because he was the player who crossed for Trevor Francis to score in the European Cup final against Swedish champions Malmo. We didn't like seeing our team lose, and I had to remind him of that when we first met. I think he was more worried that I was only eight when he was playing in a European Cup final.

It soon became obvious that Mr O'Neill was a real 'players' manager'. He knew how to approach players and talk to them. A few of the boys had lost confidence the previous season, as we hadn't won much and some of the players felt they hadn't been given a chance. Pre-season is a chance to work on those sorts of things. Bobby Petta was one example. It didn't take long for him to be transformed. Bobby never stopped being a good player, but it's hard to perform when you stop believing in yourself. When your confidence is low, you start playing to limit the mistakes you might make. You don't try anything adventurous, you play the ball back when you should be taking it forward. But playing it easy isn't always the best way. A player like Bobby will only give you his best if you are giving him the ball and asking him to take people on. Bobby is great wide on the left, attacking defenders and getting in behind defences. His game is to get at people, and now Celtic are starting to reap the rewards of that. Mr O'Neill was prepared to put confidence in Bobby and that helped him get confidence back in himself.

Our build-up to the season was really good. We played in Denmark and then had Bordeaux at Celtic Park. It was my first time back since the injury and the welcome I got from the Celtic supporters was amazing. It might only have been a friendly, but I'd been excited from the moment the alarm clock had gone off that morning. I felt really good and drove to the Park through the streets of Glasgow feeling like it was going to be a great night.

At 2–1 up, we had chances to go further ahead and that was really satisfying against a team of the quality of Bordeaux. The ball was being knocked around and the crowd were really enjoying themselves. Then we made a few defensive mistakes and ended up losing 4–2, but as I left the pitch I knew we had the sort of talent and spirit in the team to do really well. That night I told Magdalena I was going to make her proud this season. Magdalena knows quite a bit about football and she will tell me when I haven't played well. There are some times when I walk through the door and try to avoid talking about the game. She is easily my worst critic – as well as my best supporter.

The following Tuesday we played our last pre-season game, against West Ham. It's really important to put yourself to the test in the last few games before the season starts. Some teams like to play in overseas tournaments, or against smaller sides. For a team like Celtic that has big plans, you might as well put yourself up against other big sides to give yourself a standard to judge yourself by. It was good to get West Ham to the Park and it was interesting to see Paulo di Canio again. He's a really fine player, with a lot of skill, and he was very popular with the Celtic fans. I have a lot of respect for Paulo. He is a very passionate man and cares about everything he does. Some people might find his character difficult, but that is the way he is. Some players need to show their emotions.

The West Ham game was an improvement on our performance against Bordeaux and Bobby Petta had a great game. He was constantly running at defenders and seemed to be full of confidence. None of us at Celtic Park had any doubt about Bobby's ability and it was great to see him looking so up for it. Of course, we didn't know it at the time, but it was a whole new Bobby Petta we were going to see this season.

West Ham never really got into their stride, although I was impressed by Frederic Kanoute, who has great close control for such a big guy. We had a lot of possession and, just before half-time, a great ball was floated over Neil Ruddock's head for me to control and knock square to Tommy Johnson, who scored. Stilian

Petrov made it 2–0 a few minutes after half-time and, despite letting West Ham back into the match with a nicely worked goal a short time later, I don't think we ever looked like throwing the match away. Mark Fotheringham came on late in the game and immediately looked like a young guy with a good future.

At the end there was a huge cheer from the Celtic fans and I think they were impressed by the way we had gone about our task. We had taken on an English Premier League side and played really well. Of course, we knew it was only a friendly, but we still looked good.

After we beat West Ham, the manager said that we wouldn't have any excuses for not being prepared for the start of the season. He was right. We knew that we were ready, but we also knew there was a lot of pressure on us to do well. We had only won the league once in the previous 10 years and there was a lot of expectation from the fans and from the board. Fans were coming up to us and asking us to do well this season. We knew that people simply wanted us to put up a decent challenge. A new manager, new players, it's natural for people to build up their hopes, to expect results. We also expected a lot of ourselves. We'd had a good pre-season and, although that was important, I knew that it would mean absolutely nothing if we didn't get off to a winning start. Dundee United away wasn't going to be an easy game to kick-off with, but we were straining at the leash.

We went off to the hotel on Saturday afternoon. I kissed Magdalena goodbye and drove to the Park before meeting up with the rest of the boys and going on to the hotel. I tend to relax by playing PlayStation, have a bite to eat and then get an early night.

These days I always have my own room when we go to the hotel.
I used to room with Reggie Blinker, but I like to have my own room.
It's not that I'm anti-social or anything, and it can be fun sharing a
room, but it means you have to agree on everything: when to turn
on the TV, what channel to watch, when to turn it off, when to turn
out the light. I like to get to bed early, read for a bit and then sleep.
I really started reading a lot when I was injured. I got into a Swedish
detective series and I'd lie in bed desperately trying to get to the end,
so I could start the next book.

I slept well before the Dundee United game. I got up and had a
glass of orange juice. The boys were hanging around reading newspapers. We had a walk, followed by a pasta lunch and then went to the
ground. It's when you get to the last few hours before a game that you
really start concentrating on your opponents. We talked a bit about
how they might play, and I began running over in my own mind the
players that I'd be facing – de Vos, Eljofree, McCracken, Buchan –
good players who would be trying to stop me doing my job. Football
really is personal. I knew that if I could keep the defence occupied, it
would give my teammates a chance to push up and exploit the space.

Running out onto that pitch, I could hear the noisy Celtic
support singing and I knew we had to give them something to sing
about on the way home. I wasn't thinking about scoring, I just
wanted to play well and help the team to a win in our first game.
I looked over at the supporters and could see a few fans wearing
their 'Larsson' masks. I'm not sure the mask looks all that much
like me, but it is pretty funny.

As soon as the whistle went, I could feel the eagerness of my
team, everybody was looking for the ball, making runs, covering.

Nobody was hiding and you know that, when quality players are in that sort of frame of mind, you are in for a good game. After a few minutes, I managed to get into a good position, and Jackie McNamara knocked in a great ball from the right. I turned and shot but their keeper held on to it. 'Next time,' I thought, and I just hoped there would be a next time. There was, but this time Alan Combe, the United keeper, tipped my free-kick away. I gave him a look, as if to say, 'I'm going to get one past you at some point.'

The noise of the fans was amazing and they helped to drive us forward, pinning United back in their own half most of the time. Then, about 10 minutes before half-time, we managed to break through. Chris Sutton had a good shot blocked and, when the ball ran to me about 20 yards out, I lashed at it with my left foot. It was one of those efforts that you know you have hit well and just hope it's going to squeeze past the keeper. The second it hit the back of the net I wheeled away towards the section with the Celtic fans. I heard the cheer go up and there was a real feeling of relief. I always like to think there is more to my game than scoring goals, but scoring goals is still pretty good and I know it is what the fans want to see. I could just see a mass of happy, cheering faces.

We came out for the second half, just as determined, but gave away a simple goal a few minutes later. It was annoying to let them back into the game, considering how well we had been playing, but our heads didn't drop and we picked the ball out of the net and started again. Chris had the ball in the back of the net, after I pulled it back from the goal line, but the referee claimed it had gone out. It hadn't. Moments like that really annoy me. It's frustrating when you are working hard to get a result and a bad decision goes against you. But there's nothing you can do about it. You just have to swallow it.

We had a few more efforts after that and then, about 20 minutes from the end, Stephane Mahe shot across the face of the goal and Chris was there to knock it in. It was great for him, his first goal on his debut, and you could see from his reaction that he enjoyed it. The fans went mad and I knew there was a good chance the game was ours. We were playing well and just had to keep going. I wanted to keep attacking, so that we didn't give United a chance to come back at us. These days you have to be prepared to battle for 95 minutes and not start thinking the game is over. The final whistle was a welcome relief and we saluted the fans before making our way back to a jubilant dressing room.

There were a lot of happy faces, and the manager was shaking everybody by the hand and slapping them on the back. The point was we had won, and done so with a bit of style and confidence. I was about to get changed when Mr O'Neill came up to me. 'Henrik, before the game I thought you were a good player, but I was wrong.' He paused and then smiled. 'You're a great player,' he said. I was a bit embarrassed. I know not to get too carried away with that sort of praise because people can get quite excited when they're happy, and if I turned in a couple of bad performances it could all change. Having said that, I respected Mr O'Neill a lot and it did make me feel good to be paid that sort of compliment.

During the drive home, I listened to a bit of the Notorious B.I.G. on CD and ran the game over in my head. It had been good, no doubt about that, and the big English guy up front was a real pleasure to have in the side. I could see there were ways our games could complement each other. It was only one game, but to start with an away win, with that style, was great. I thought about the problems of the previous season, and could hardly believe how good I felt.

My car slid into the driveway and I was home in Bothwell. Magdalena had let Jordan stay up so that I could put him to bed. It's one of the things I really love doing. We play around for a bit and then I pretend to get stern and lie him down. It's a great way to unwind after a game and get the adrenaline out of my system. He's a good kid and makes me laugh a lot.

Once he was asleep, I went downstairs to have a bite to eat and relax. Magdalena knew I'd played quite well, so I didn't have to worry about getting a telling off from her.

'How do you feel?' She asked me.

'I feel pretty good,' I said. 'This isn't a bad team.'

chapter four
into europe

It's strange how your feelings can change so much in just 24 hours. I'd gone to bed after the Dundee United game on a real high. We'd had a pretty good start to the season and I was feeling sharp. Then, the next day, Marc Rieper announced that he was going to quit the game. The toe injury that had been troubling him for so long had finally beaten him. It was a blow for Celtic and for me personally because Marc and I had become close friends.

The fact is that I'd known for a little while that he had decided to call it a day, but when such an announcement is made public it really hits you. As a footballer you know that either you or any one of your teammates could be forced out of the game at any time, but that still doesn't prepare you for when it happens.

Marc had tried everything, he'd been seeing specialists and he'd had three separate operations. After all that, though, he simply had to accept that he'd lost the battle. A Danish international, he had been so important to the Celtic defence in the 1997–98 season, totally solid alongside Alan Stubbs. Marc's a real character, always up for a laugh, and I felt very sad that such a nice guy was going to have to stop playing the game he loved. He had really enjoyed himself at Celtic.

The life of a footballer means that you make a lot of friends, but you also spend quite a lot of time saying goodbye to people. Rieps is one of those people who I'm just glad I got a chance to meet and play football with. I've kept in touch and we see each other from time to time. We still have a good laugh and get in a round of golf when we can.

Despite losing Marc, the fact that Martin O'Neill had started strengthening the squad, and also that a few players who had been on the sidelines the previous season had been given a lift and were now back in the reckoning, meant that there was a lot of competition for first team places. The manager was still settling on his team and every place was up for grabs. And that inevitably meant some people would be disappointed. I have no idea what goes on in the heads of other players, so I don't know exactly what the lads who were on the sidelines were thinking. One of the challenges of playing at a big club with a strong squad is that you may not play. Nobody has an automatic right to play, but I know, after my experiences at Feyenoord, how frustrating it can be when you think you should be playing, but find yourself on the bench. Of course, players who haven't been happy for a while hope that a new manager will bring about a change in their fortunes.

Players like Mark Burchill and Eyal Berkovic were obviously unhappy because they wanted to play football and they felt they weren't being given the opportunities. Both are good players and were anxious about their places. You can read a lot about players being unhappy in situations like that, but it can get blown out of proportion, so people start to think that there are problems at the club. But that isn't the case. It is the most natural thing for a footballer to want to play, but a player's unhappiness on the bench doesn't necessarily affect the spirit in the team. If players want to talk to you, you listen, but you just get on and try to do your best for the club and to retain your place in the team.

Our win against Dundee United had been a great start to the season, but we were determined not to get carried away. All the players and the management staff were out to build on that result. Our next opponents were Motherwell and after them we would be facing Jeunesse Esch of Luxembourg in qualifying for the UEFA Cup. Both were incredibly important games, Motherwell because it was a chance to start a run of league wins and Jeunesse because it was our passport into Europe proper. For a club like Celtic, it is really important to play in Europe. It gives the players valuable experience, the supporters an opportunity to watch some great games, and the club a lot of exposure. Playing in Europe is also a chance to bring in extra money which can be used to strengthen the squad.

Having said that, I'm not in favour of a European league. I know some people say it is inevitable, but there are a lot of things to consider before you go ahead with a change of that magnitude, including what the supporters want. I think it would be unfair on them. Celtic fans love travelling away, and we get tremendous support when we play away, but you couldn't expect fans to travel abroad every second week, it would be impossible financially. They make an incredible effort to follow us around Scotland, but Europe would be too much.

The second reason is that I don't believe a European league would be as enjoyable to play in. It's great to be part of one of the big European competitions because it is not an everyday thing.

It's special, you look forward to it and it's a bonus on top of your usual work. If you were playing European sides all the time, though. it would lose some of its interest and excitement.

To be honest, there is a third reason. I travel enough as it is, both with Celtic and with Sweden. I'm happy to do so, it's my job and it's an honour, but I am away from home quite a lot and that means I miss my wife and son. I know that we get a pretty good life in return for the few sacrifices we make, but I really don't think it is fair on footballers' families to be dragging them away even more than they are at the moment.

A European league may be something that will come in the future, I know there is a lot of interest in it and, obviously, if I'm called upon by my club to take part, I will. But I think there is a long way to go before it could actually happen and the football powers should think long and hard before they make any decisions about it.

The prospect of Motherwell was tough enough. We'd lost twice to them the previous season and they obviously felt they had a bit of a jinx over us. If you haven't done well against a certain side, it does make you more eager to get a result, to do better and to prove that they don't have any special ability to beat you. In the run-up to the game, there was a lot of speculation about Mark Bosnich coming to the club from Manchester United, and that Neil Lennon was on the point of signing from Leicester, but we were just concentrating on our preparation for the game. The politics and speculation sort of pass you by as a player; that is the job of the manager.

Obviously Mr O'Neill had not had much opportunity to study the other teams in the league, so he wasn't trying to give us the low-down on the opposition. He was more interested in getting us to play to his style and to believe in ourselves. And it was already starting to work. Lubo Moravcik was really eager to get out and play against Motherwell, having been suspended for the opening game. My pal Johan Mjallby was also anxious to make the team after having missed the first game through injury. If anything, we were in a better position for this game that we had been for Dundee United.

Of course, the game didn't turn out quite as we expected. We managed to get a 1–0 victory, thanks to a goal by Stilian Petrov, but the referee sent off three players, including Chris Sutton and Jackie McNamara for us. It was a tough game, very physical, and I don't think Motherwell set out to attack at all. Their plan was to get players behind the ball and tackle hard.

Given the way the game developed, we were lucky to get a breakthrough early on. Stilian scored after 10 minutes and we spent most of the rest of the game trying to break down some incredibly stubborn resistance. Chris's first booking was incredible. He appeared to get pulled down but ended up being the one getting the yellow card. Jackie then got booked twice for two innocuous challenges and Chris got a second booking for a 50-50 tackle. With the team reduced to nine men, the boss sent on Johan to close things up, and Paul Lambert came into his own. He battled for every ball and used it intelligently to keep possession, and that, along with the magnificent supporters, got us through the game, which included a tortuous five minutes of extra time.

It was the first of a number of games we won by a single goal and showed we could battle and hold on. It's not really the 4–0 victories that win league titles, it's the games you win by a single goal, when you might have drawn or lost. The Motherwell game was an indication of the sort of character that we were to show throughout the season.

After that battle, it was almost a relief to be heading off to Luxembourg for the game against Jeunesse. We travelled out the day before and stayed in a fine hotel. Celtic are particularly good at making sure the team stays somewhere quiet, that has all the facilities you could want. It's a strange life, travelling to different countries and mostly being able to remember them only by the look of the hotel lobby. Sometimes you do get a glimpse of the country from the coach and it makes you want to come back and have a proper look.

We arrived in Luxembourg amid warm August sunshine and we had a short training session early in the day to loosen up. Later, sitting in the changing room before the game, I was totally aware that it was a match we had to win and win convincingly. We needed to progress in Europe, but it wasn't as simple as that. A lot of people would be looking at how we performed against a supposedly 'small' side. The manager drummed in the message that you can't be complacent against anyone, there are no easy teams out there any more and we don't have the right to win just because we are Celtic. It all sounds obvious, but you do have to keep repeating it to yourself so that you don't get carried away by all the newspapers' expectations of a massacre. Teams like Jeunesse may not be the strongest in the world going forward, but it's the easiest thing in football to be negative and destructive.

I wasn't nervous as such, I don't get massively nervous, but I was itching to get out and get on with the job. It was quite a small stadium but as always there was a great travelling support and,

Feyenoord was my big break into top flight European football.

Top: I remember as if it were yesterday the goal I scored in the 4-1 win over Bulgaria to clinch third place in the 1994 World Cup.

Above: Getting your hands on a trophy like this one, for Feyenoord, is every kid's dream.

Above right: Winning the league in 1998 was fantastic for us and stopped Rangers' run of nine titles in a row.

Opposite: The world seemed to stop at this moment, when I broke my leg against Lyon in the UEFA Cup.

Top: It was a massive relief to beat Dundee 2–1 in the first game of the season.
Above: Everyone was waiting to see how we performed against Rangers – we beat them 6-2.

Top: Hibs were a threat all season, but beating them 3–0 in September was a big boost.
Above: It didn't take Chris Sutton and I long to strike up a successful partnership.

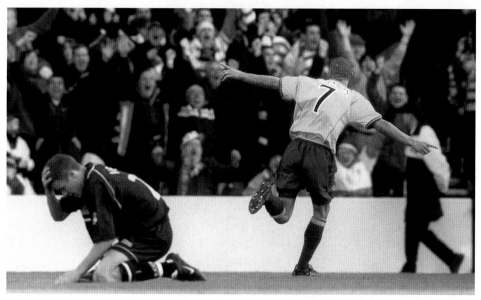

Top left: Going out at home to Bordeaux was the real low point of the season.

Below left: In February we faced playing Rangers twice in one week. This 3-1 CIS Cup semi-final win set us up nicely.

Top: The CIS Cup Final was our first chance of silverware – and it was great to get the first goal.

Above: Don't ask me why I do aeroplane impressions after scoring, I just do!

Top: The third goal of the CIS Cup Final against Kilmarnock was my favourite of the season.
Left: It was great to see those green and white ribbons on the CIS Cup.

as soon as we went out onto the pitch, we could hear all those Glaswegian voices. Straight from the whistle we tried to attack and get things going, but for one reason or another it seemed difficult to get into our stride. We hadn't played great football against Motherwell, although I think we had battled brilliantly, and there was a bit of a hangover from that. Of course, in the days leading up to the game there had been mention of the Inverness Cally result. As long as football is played in Scotland, people will remember Celtic losing that match. But anyone who expected a similar upset wasn't banking on the faith in our side.

After a bit of a struggle, we managed to get a goal and that settled us down. By the end, it was 4–0 and we knew the tie was effectively over. Chris and I had worked quite well together and I was really starting to appreciate his qualities. I wouldn't say that we had developed an understanding yet, that would come with time, but we were learning how to bring each other into the game. Chris is very strong and it helps the team to know that, if the defence is under a bit of pressure, they can punt the ball up towards Chris and he can hold it up. I always take up a position where the defence can get the ball out to me, but I soon realized it was a job that Chris could do far better than me. It is a physical game and you always benefit from having a big, strong player around.

We returned from Luxembourg knowing that we had done the job expected of us. The return leg was a bit of a formality and the manager chose to rest a few players, including me. I didn't enjoy being on the sidelines. There are really no circumstances when I wouldn't rather be out on the Park. Of course, there are days, as in any job, when you feel tired, but once you are on the pitch, you realize how lucky you are to be able to do this for a living. There are all those people up in the stands who would give anything to be down there with a Celtic shirt on their back. They are the ones you think about when you feel a bit tired going into training. I also think back to when I was a teenager with Hogaborg in my home town.

At that time, just when I thought I'd made it as a footballer, suddenly my career seemed to come to a standstill. I found it difficult to concentrate on training and I was having too much of a good time outside football. Although I knew I needed to keep working hard, I wasn't as committed as I should have been and, for the second time in my career, I could easily have drifted out of the game. I stopped believing that football was going to be my life. By the time I turned 21 it seemed that I might have missed the boat. Then one day at work, I got a call saying the local professional side Helsingborgs IF were interested in me. A friend drove me over to the ground and I signed immediately for £300 a month without bonuses. I was working in a youth centre at the time and I suppose I could have ended up in some sort of social work. I'm sure that it's a great career, but for me it's difficult to compare with running out at Celtic Park.

The boys put seven past Jeunesse in the home leg, with Mark Burchill and Bobby Petta having a great match. The two young players, Simon Lynch and Colin Healy, gained some valuable experience and Eyal Berkovic played beautifully, weighing in with a couple of goals. I've heard people claim that Eyal is a difficult guy, but I have never had any problems with him. He's a strong competitor, sure, and he wants to be involved. He can be outspoken, too, but he just wants to put his point across. Some people are quiet, others let you know what they are thinking all the time. You'll always find both types at a football club.

It was a good feeling to know that we had silenced the doubters with the game against Jeunesse, and would be making progress in the UEFA Cup. At the end of the game I walked over to congratulate Bobby Petta on a great performance and he had a huge smile on his face. Amazingly, even though we'd had the tie more or less sewn up from the first leg, there were more than 40,000 people crammed into Paradise. Many players will go their whole career without playing in front of a home crowd that size. For a Celtic player, it is usual to have 60,000 fans watching you, and it becomes hard to imagine what it's like for other teams. I know I'd be happy to play every game at home, but somehow I don't think the other clubs would agree to it.

Between the Jeunesse matches we picked up another couple of good results, beating Kilmarnock 2–1 and Hearts 4–2. The Kilmarnock game was a bit scrappy and, as we came off the pitch, we knew we would have to do better if we were going to make a real impression this season. But we knuckled down, even when we had gone a goal behind early on, and made the tackles when they counted. I think we were all aware that we had lacked a bit of fighting spirit the season before and the feeling was that that wasn't going to be the thing that held us back now.

We were training hard and the whole team was starting to look really sharp. Even the players who were rumoured to be wanting to get away were committed to the cause. Obviously, we knew that the manager was still looking at other players and there was constant speculation in the press about all sorts of people, but the manager was keeping his head down. He was probably getting a little tired of the constant speculation. Every time he was interviewed, he had to deny an interest in some player. The Mark Bosnich rumours were becoming especially intense.

We were playing so many games in the early part of the season that there was no time for anything other than playing and training. Most of the time I was too tired to do much else and there certainly wasn't any golf being played. An occasional meal out was about it. Magdalena and I had bought another Rhodesian Ridgeback, called Cimba, and when we were playing two games a week, walking Cimba was just about the only time I got out of the house other than to go to work. He's a big, gentle giant with a bark that is certainly a great deal worse than his bite and we know we can trust him entirely. Jordan climbs all over him, which is pretty funny to watch.

Against Hearts, Chris was really starting to get his act together and scored twice in five minutes in the first half. He'd missed the Kilmarnock game through suspension and in the dressing room before this match he looked very determined. He's quite an easy-going guy, but gets incredibly focused just before going on the pitch. His first goal was a great header from an inch-perfect cross by Bobby Petta. Then he got on the end of Bobby's free-kick to flick the ball past Niemi in the Hearts goal.

An understanding was beginning to develop between Chris and me, and I scored from a move with him, only to have the goal ruled offside. Then, about five minutes before half-time, I made it 3–0 with a rather lucky goal. Lubo took a free kick which was cleared as far as Paul Lambert. Paul took a shot and I managed to get a boot on the end of it to deflect it past the keeper. It wasn't the prettiest goal ever, but I was in the right place at the right time, and I've always believed that is one of the most important attributes of being a striker. At least, that's what I said to the guys in the changing room after the game.

Hearts are a good side and they were fighting hard after the break. They pulled back to 3–1 and then, when we scored a fourth through Lubo, they got another. It was one of those games that swings one way and then the other and you just want to get a couple of goals in front to give yourself some breathing space. For the last 20 minutes, Hearts threw everything at us, but we kept tackling and trying to play football. When we got the chance, we were knocking the ball around and, when we had to, we fought.

We were getting into a winning habit. That evening I sat thinking about how we were playing, and, although we'd now won six games out of six and had a perfect 12 points in the league, I wasn't that happy with my own performance. I had played okay, but I felt I could do a lot better. I was over anxious because we had a new manager and I wanted him to be aware of how much playing for Celtic meant to me. The boys had been playing well and helped me a great deal, but I just wanted to make sure I had a place on merit. Magdalena could see I was worried about something. 'I don't know,' I said, 'I just don't think I'm doing myself justice.' Talking about it helped me make up my mind to go to see the manager and talk him through my concerns.

The following day I asked to see Mr O'Neill and he called me into his office. It was the same office that I'd walked into to ask Kenny Dalglish to give me the chance to play in Euro 2000, and that memory was still fresh in my mind. The manager was in a good mood, smiling and happy with the way things were going. He'd already said that it was still too early to make any long-term decisions about the playing staff, but I was determined to let him know that I wanted to be a part of his plans.

He invited me to sit down and asked me how things were going. I told him I didn't think I was at my best yet and I wanted to make sure that I was doing enough for the team. I didn't want to let Celtic down. He looked at me and smiled again. 'Look, Henrik,' he said, 'the fact is that I'm really pleased with the way you're playing. I know what you've been through and I'm not expecting you to have the greatest touch in the world just at the moment. I think you're doing great for the team and I reckon in a short time you'll be back to your best. Just keep doing what you're doing and I don't think there will be too many complaints.'

It was exactly what I needed to hear. I'm not sure if Mr O'Neill was being totally straight, or whether he was just trying to boost my confidence, but I felt much better as I walked from his office. I'm like any player who needs to have a bit of reassurance from time to time. Out on the pitch I might look complacent, but that is never the case. You only ever feel as good as your last performance and when you don't think you've played well, the only thing you want to do is get back out on the pitch and show what you're capable of.

It was a crucial time to have my confidence lifted. Just around the corner was a match that would show us how far we had come. The first Old Firm game of the season was only eight days away and already I could hear the crowd warming up.

chapter five
the old firm

Nothing in my football career came anywhere near to preparing me for the Old Firm match. Of course, I'd played derby matches before, and in Holland the Feyenoord v Ajax game was a pretty big event. There were a couple of times when Ajax fans had used the Feyenoord coach for target practice and there was always a lot of excitement surrounding the match. But it didn't begin to compare with the meeting of the Old Firm.

I know people are aware of the Celtic v Rangers game all over Europe and it consumes the Scottish sport pages. Anyone who lives in Glasgow gets caught up in it in some way, but you only really experience it if you are part of the whole thing, as a player, as a supporter or as part of the club staff.

It's not a game you have to psyche yourself up for. As soon as the whistle goes on the last game before an Old Firm clash, everybody starts asking you for your thoughts on the forthcoming clash. The papers are full of nothing else and people stop you in the street to talk about it. It's a welcome pressure because it's what football is all about at this level. I'm usually quite a laid- back sort of guy, but my adrenaline is pumping in the days before we take on Rangers.

When the season kicked off it was Rangers who we were looking at as the team to beat. They were the standard that any team in the Scottish Premier League had to aim for if they wanted to win something. It hurts at Celtic if you find yourself in the shadow of the team in blue and, when this season kicked off, we knew we were seen as being firmly in that shadow. Over the summer, Rangers hadn't lost any of their best players and they'd brought a few in, so they were probably even stronger than the year before.

The fact that I was born in Sweden doesn't mean that I don't understand how much this game means to the club and to the supporters. Victory means we can walk with our heads held high, defeat is unthinkable. The week before our first meeting with Rangers this season was like any other pre-Old Firm week: chaotic.

We'd only just started the season and were getting into our stride when suddenly Rangers appeared, ready to spoil the party that we'd been having since that first victory at Dundee United. Although there were a number of sides that could offer a challenge, this was the game that everybody was looking at to judge the Celtic team's strength. To be honest, I don't think it's a game you can ever predict. Form counts for very little once you kick off. All you can do is battle until the final whistle, with your ears ringing from the noise and the sound of your heart thumping in your chest.

A couple of days before the game, I picked up the morning paper just to get a hint of what was being said. It was full of stories about the guys who were making their first Old Firm appearances and how they would handle the big occasion. I knew that feeling. My first had been away at Ibrox and I remember running out on to the pitch and being hit with a wall of sound that felt like it could have blown me right back down the tunnel. It's something that you never get used to, but at least you get to the point where you know what to expect. I lost that first game, and the feeling of disappointment among the players and fans was something that I filed away in my memory. If I ever did need an incentive to make me play well against Rangers, I would just pull that memory out and take a long look at it.

On our side, Chris Sutton, Tommy Johnson and Joos Valgaeren were all facing their Old Firm baptisms of fire. It was funny, because Joos had been quoted as saying he was sick of all the hype surrounding the match. I think he just couldn't believe how much attention there was and that you couldn't escape it. By the end of the week he just wanted to get the game on.

Even my friends back in Sweden ask me what it's like to play in a game like this and I struggle to describe it to them. How can you convey the experience of a noise so loud that you can barely hear your teammates shouting right next to you? How can you explain the feeling when you see the passion on the faces of fans who have put all their faith in you?

At one time we only ever went into a hotel for away games or any games against Rangers. That's changed now and we always stay away before a game. On paper our preparation for every league game is the same now, but the truth is the Rangers game still gets special treatment.

So, on Saturday 26 August, I said goodbye to Jordan, Magdalena and Cimba and drove to the hotel at Dunblane. The radio was on in the car and I had to switch it over from sports programmes so that I could relax during the drive. While I was stopped in traffic, a bunch of kids who'd been kicking a ball about, noticed me and ran up to the wire mesh fence a few yards away. They were shouting and chanting and smiling, so I wound the window down to wave. Unfortunately, now that I could hear them, I realized they were little Rangers fans and their chants weren't complimentary. Still, it was just a little bit of stick and quite funny. As the lights changed I gave them my biggest smile and held up four fingers to indicate how many goals we were going to score and that sent them into a shouting frenzy as I drove away.

All the guys were in the hotel, milling around and chatting. It's good to be with the team just before a big game. Only the other players can really know what it's like, so you want to be with people who are sharing that feeling. Everyone sits down to a late lunch and the usual rituals and jokes are gone over for the millionth time.

I didn't really want to talk about the game and that seemed fine with everybody else, as we covered each other's personal habits and anything other than the match. After dinner everyone splits up to relax. A few of the boys take books or papers and lounge around reading. I decided to challenge Johan Mjallby to a game on the PlayStation and give him a thorough beating at ice hockey. At about 10pm I sloped off to my room to lie down and read a bit before going to sleep. Some players are happy to stay up quite late the night before a game, but I'm definitely not, I'm a big fan of sleep.

I was woken by somebody knocking on the door to tell me it was 10am. There was a pre-match get-together at 10.45, so I just had time for a shower and a glass of juice. The chat is usually just a broad plan of the way we are going to play, what we can expect and what is expected of us. I started to run over in my mind the players

I would be facing. There is no point in trying to prepare for each game by analyzing who you are going to be up against in tiny detail. You don't adapt your game to suit every single opponent, but it is important to have a broad idea of their strengths and weaknesses.

The Rangers defence would be strong and skilful. I knew that players like Konterman, Ricksen, Numan, Wilson and Amoruso all had a lot of ability. But what I also knew was that you have to attack them hard, run at them, keep the ball coming in from all angles and mix the play up. It was no secret that we were starting to use our wings very effectively and the strikers were feeding off a lot of good balls played into the box. I knew this game would be no different. I would get the service and so would Chris, so it was up to us to make sure we were getting into good positions.

Rangers had a number of dangerous guys who you had to respect. Barry Ferguson isn't exactly a favourite among Celtic fans, but he is always a determined opponent, and at that stage of the season Giovanni van Bronckhorst was playing really well for them.

I felt sorry for Gio when he suffered a long-term injury, because he's a quality player and I know what it's like to be out of the game for a long time. He was inspirational to their midfield and I'm sure they missed him a lot when he was out. We have become friends over the years, which I suppose might seem strange to some people who know of the Old Firm rivalry. The fact is that out on that pitch there is intense rivalry between every Celtic player and every Rangers player. You want nothing more than to win for your club and the supporters. I'm here to play football and my commitment to Celtic Football Club is total, but off the pitch we become just like anyone else.

In the hours before a game there are loads of thoughts that
go through my mind. I'm not planning as such, but I am having
thoughts about how I want to play and imagining situations.
I suppose the only way I can really describe it is that I'm having a
preview of the game in my mind and imagining what I would do if
certain things were to happen. I wanted to tie up their defence as
much as possible, because I knew that, if they were having to
double up on me, I could create space for our midfield to come
through. I felt Chris was well up for the game and I was sure he
would be able to create all sorts of trouble for Rangers at the back.

After the pre-match ,we all go for a walk, to relax and loosen up,
and then it's off to lunch. My pre-match meal is always spaghetti
bolognese. I love pasta anyway, but it invariably seems like the right
thing to have before a game. I'm pretty lucky in that I can eat almost
anything. Of course, I don't ,but I don't have to worry about having
the odd burger from time to time. Footballers are more and more into
their diet and nutrition, and everybody seems to be eating bananas.
I just think that so long as you don't have too much greasy or sweet
stuff you'll be fine. I'm certainly not picky with my diet and I never
feel bad. Like a lot of top clubs, Celtic has a nutritionist, but I tend
only to visit for specific advice, as when I was injured.

The drive to the ground is the time when everyone really
starts talking about the match and you can feel the tension and
anticipation rising. I look out the window and imagine it's a few
hours later and that we've won the game. That's a good feeling and
one I want to have for real.

From inside the stands, you can really hear the noise of the fans
above. You can feel it in your chest and it almost makes the stadium

shake. By the time you run out on the pitch, the adrenaline is pumping so hard through your veins that you can hear the blood pounding in your ears.

Our game plan was to keep the pace up, use the physical presence of players like Chris and Joos, get the ball out to Bobby and Lubo as much as possible and battle from the first to last whistle. Of course, our game plan didn't include the possibility that we would score in the first minute. But that is exactly what happened, and it stunned us as much as anyone else.

Alan Stubbs knocked the ball down to me after Lubo had put in a great cross. I took a swing at it and as the ball was going wide, Chris was there to stick out a foot and put it away. There was the tiniest moment when we all paused. I'm sure it's my imagination, but it seemed like the crowd went quiet just for a second and then the whole place erupted. I don't think I've ever heard the supporters so loud. Sixty thousand fans were going crazy and it was everything we could do not to go a bit crazy too.

Everyone was just looking at each other and saying, 'Okay, let's get back to it now.' We had to keep calm and keep playing football. Rangers came right back at us and we had a couple of narrow escapes, which helped to bring our boots right back down to earth. Then it happened again.

Another cross from Lubo and Stilian Petrov headed home. It was madness. There were seven minutes gone and we were 2–0 up. You're not quite sure if it's all a dream and any second you'll hear the knock on the door to tell you it's 10am.

The crowd were loving it and, when Paul Lambert made it 3–0 I thought the roof was about to come off the stadium. I was desperate to get in on the scoring and opportunities were coming my way, but for a while it looked like I was never going to put any of the half-chances away.

My first real chance came after we were 3–0 up. Jonathan Gould punted the ball upfield to Lubo, who knocked it over the top to me on the left side of the penalty box. As Stefan Klos came out I thought I'd step over the ball, drag it past him and have a clear shot. Somehow I missed the drag back and the ball got caught up underneath me. The next moment the keeper was on top of it. I got another chance when Bobby Petta's shot was knocked away and the ball fell to me in the area. As it was in the air, I threw myself forward and just tried to guide it in, but all I succeeded in doing was missing the target completely.

Of course, when you're 3–0 up, you don't kick yourself over misses like that as much you would if it were 0–0 in the last minute. But one of my jobs is to score goals and I don't like missing opportunities. As I walked away from the goal I was cursing myself for not taking an extra half second to set myself right. But I had to shake myself out of the disappointment and get back on track. 'Okay, you'll get another chance and you'll put that one away.' The beauty of the game for a striker is the anticipation of those moments when you get a chance to score. I could wait.

Unfortunately, it was Claudio Reyna for Rangers who got the next chance and he scored with a header past Gouldie. Still, we went in at half-time feeling pretty satisfied with the job we had done so far. We could never have imagined we would be 3–1 up at this point and we even felt there was more to come. Of course, there is a small voice in your mind that's saying, 'Well, if you can score three goals in one half, so can they.' Even if they were to get one more goal back, it would start to become tense again. But that thought can help. It stops you getting carried away with yourself and keeps your work rate and concentration going.

Everyone was refuelling: some people have a snack at half time – bananas, obviously, and even chocolate – but I just drink. If it's a bit cold, I'll have some hot tea without milk or sugar, otherwise just some juice, but today I just wanted to get out there again. As I sipped my juice, the manager was telling us to stay calm and just keep on playing the way we were.

We started the second half much as we'd started the first – going forward – and it wasn't long before I was able to get the goal that had been eluding me. I've had a lot of people say to me since that they think it was one of the best goals they've seen, and I have to say I enjoyed it myself.

Gouldie hit a long clearance which I could see was going to Chris. He did brilliantly to chest it down to me and I took it in my stride. I knew I had Tugay on my right shoulder, so I started running right and then cut left again. I saw Konterman coming towards me and I could also see that there was space behind him. I can't explain why I nutmegged him, it just seemed the thing to do at that moment. I had to get past him and, from the angle I was running at, that was about the only thing I could do.

Once past Konterman, I could see the keeper coming out to close me down, so I immediately decided to lift it over him... and it went in. As soon as I hit it, I thought it was going in, it felt totally right when it left my boot. But there were a few moments when it seemed to be on a strange curve that would take it over the bar. In a split second it reached the top of its trajectory and started dipping, and then I knew it was a goal. The cheers started at about the same moment as I turned away and a huge sense of relief washed over me.

It was a great game and to score a goal like that in it was a special feeling. Surely, now we were home and dry. Of course, we had to give the fans one more scare. Rod Wallace went down in the area and Billy Dodds scored from the spot. For a moment we felt a little flat to see a small piece of our hard work undone, but one of the things that has become a hallmark of this season is the commitment of the players, and we weren't about to let the manager down on this occasion.

A few minutes later Johan Mjallby won a free-kick, which Bobby curled over beautifully. I looked around and realized I was practically unmarked. I think Barry Ferguson was directly behind me, but I managed to get up and put enough of my head on the ball to glance it into the far corner. Although I'm not very tall, I've always been pretty good with my head, ever since I was a kid. I can jump quite high, but a lot of it is timing and being prepared to get up among the bigger guys. I do a bit of upper body strength work, just to be able to hold my own in those contests. I might not be the strongest guy around, but I'm strong enough.

The other thing about heading a ball is to be totally prepared. You have to get position yourself where you think the ball will come and then have the awareness to know what you're going to do if it does arrive. You see some players make a run, then turn to find that the ball is about to reach them, and it bounces off the top of their head.

By now the Celtic fans were singing, 'Always Look on the Bright Side of Life'. Rangers' misery was further compounded when Barry

Ferguson was sent off for a second bookable offence. It wasn't a dirty game. Tough and physical, yes, but not dirty. Ferguson paid the price for being totally committed. And then the final nail in Rangers' coffin came in the dying seconds when Chris steered a low cross by Stephane Mahe into the net. The referee's whistle brought a wave of elation and we all turned to the supporters. You could almost feel the years of suffering fall away. Not only were we on a great run, but we'd beaten Rangers in spectacular fashion.

The changing room was buzzing. The manager was delighted. We'd beaten our biggest rivals. No, we'd destroyed our biggest rivals, with skill and determination. We knew that the Celtic supporters, the staff at the Park, could all get up the next day and have a smile on their faces. It is amazing how much pleasure you can give people when you are a footballer, and as I lay in bed that night I was pleased with what we'd achieved. Our fans have had a lot of stick to put up with over the last decade, but they knew, for a while at least, that now it was their turn to take the Mickey.

The next day it was easy to get up. I didn't feel tired at all and, although it was a day off, I would happily have gone into training. Despite how good we felt, we knew it was only one win. An important one, obviously, but one that would mean little at the end of the season if we started losing. We knew, and the manager reminded us, that we couldn't get carried away. And we made sure that we didn't. Instead, we gave ourselves a brief time to enjoy the result and then, as ever, it was on to the next game.

chapter six
the big disappointment

Just inside the main entrance to Celtic Park is a plaque which reads 'Celtic Football and Athletic Company Limited', under which are the dates 1888–1988. I pass it most days. To me, coming from Sweden where the first professional club was formed in 1999, it is something special to be surrounded by so much history.

Of course, nearly all Celtic fans know the history of the club, how it was founded by Brother Wilfrid, who was inspired by Hibernian in Edinburgh, and who saw it as a way of raising money for a children's charity. They are also aware of how Celtic was the first British club to win the European Cup, with that famous 2–1 victory over Milan in Lisbon in 1967. For me, the realisation that I was part of something special, some incredible tradition, took place over the first few months after I moved to Glasgow.

As you wander around the club, you are faced with old pictures, pennants from games, trophies and memorabilia spanning the whole of the last century. And, of course, it's not all in the past. The history of Celtic is being written every day. Each time we step out onto the pitch, we can add a few words and we know that if we do well, we could get a whole chapter to ourselves.

You only have to look at players like our club captain, Tommy Boyd – who almost glows with pride when he puts on the hooped shirt – players who have grown up with Celtic in their blood, to get an idea of what it is all about. But even though the likes of me and Joos, Lubo and the rest of the so-called 'imports' haven't had that background, we still understand how Celtic is different from other clubs.

I have a huge respect for the things that Celtic has achieved on the pitch over the years, but for me the thing that sets this club apart from every other is the supporters. I love Celtic and when I think of Celtic, it is the fans that I think of first.

Of course, Celtic is a big, attractive club to support ,and often has the potential to win trophies, but the fans have stuck with it through the tough times too. Many of the people who now fill the stadium to capacity every home game were also there when we were struggling to keep up with Rangers and not winning anything.

When you turn up at an away ground, be it in Scotland or for a European match, and you hear the songs and chants of the Celtic fans, it is an unbelievable feeling. There are grounds we go to where, if you closed your eyes, you would think you were at Celtic Park.

In the days following the win against Rangers, you could spot a Celtic fan at 100 yards by the smile on his face, and we were eager to keep it that way. It was my best ever start to a campaign, totally unbelievable: seven wins out of seven in all competitions and six goals to my name. Our next challenge was Raith Rovers in the CIS Cup at the Park. Okay, so it might have seemed like a bit of a step down from the passion of the Old Firm match, but it was still a game we had to go out and win.

The last thing that goes through your mind when you are playing those early rounds is winning the cup. All you see is the next game. That is how we approached Raith Rovers. A small club, yes, but one with a lot of pride and the will to knock mighty Celtic off its high horse. I know what it's like. When I played for my home town team in Sweden, we were desperate to do well against the bigger, better-known sides. If you managed to draw a team from a higher division in the cup, you'd be polishing your boots the night before. It would be the biggest game of your season and you'd want to prove that, just because your club was small, it didn't mean you were bad players.

I was actually rested for the Raith game and I watched as the boys did a totally professional job to win 4–0. Raith were a good side and were certainly no push-over, but again the boys showed the total commitment that had come to typify Mr O'Neill's team.

A bigger threat came in our next match when we entertained Hibernian at Celtic Park. Hibs had had a great start to the season too. There are normally one or two clubs every year, in addition to Celtic and Rangers, who put up a good fight and challenge for the honours. This season, it soon became obvious that Hibs were going to be one of those sides.

I think their real strength was based on a good passing game. They had a number of players who could put teammates away and the threat could come from either side of the pitch. There was also a real belief throughout the team that I hadn't seen before in a Hibs side and that is obviously a compliment to Alex McLeish, who has built a good unit there.

We didn't start brilliantly, but as the game wore on we began to impose ourselves. Joos and Lubo were playing well and holding things together. I felt good, it was one of those games where your touch is sure, and I was working hard to link up and play people in. Even when you're in a high-pressure game, it can be a lot of fun if things are going right for you. Jackie McNamara was causing Hibs all sorts of problems on our right wing, and Lubo had a great shot tipped over the bar.

Then, after about a quarter of an hour, Alan Thompson was brought down in the area by the Hibs keeper. As soon as he hit the turf, I started to walk towards the penalty spot. It was my job. I wouldn't say I like taking penalties, but somebody has to do it and the odds are stacked in your favour – unlike many scoring chances. I put it away and I think it helped to settle us down a bit.

Hibs were still in the game and as the fans urged us on we were desperate to put it beyond their reach. The next goal was a bit special, a great move that left me with a simple finish. Lubo took a corner which was cleared as far as Paul Lambert. Paul played a fantastic first-time ball back to Lubo, one of the best passes I've seen, and Lubo crossed again. I got on the end of it to head home and give us the cushion we needed.

A little while later there was a murmur of excitement in the crowd and we realized that Dundee must have equalized in their game against Rangers. Boosted by that, we continued to press and, right at the end of the game, I passed to Paul, who knocked the ball square to Mark Burchill for a shot which he buried. The fans were singing, 'We shall not be moved', and we knew it would take a lot to shift us now.

With things still going pretty much our way in the league, it was a good time to turn our attention to Europe. Having disposed of Jeunesse in the qualifying round, the real business of the UEFA Cup was about to begin.

Celtic had not managed to mount a proper assault on Europe since I had come to the club and we were eager to change that this year. In fact, the club hadn't reached the second round proper for 17 years. I don't know why, but what I do know is that you play a totally different game in two-legged European competitions. The basic plan is to try to snatch a goal in the away leg and not concede one at home. It sounds simple, but it isn't. In some ways it's like a game of chess, trying to out-think your opponent and decide if he is going to be a little bit adventurous.

We had drawn Helsinki at home in the first leg of the first round proper, which we were quite happy with. While everyone is always saying you can't underestimate any opponent these days, it wasn't the toughest start and it gave us a chance to get into our stride. As I've said before, I regard Europe as an exciting extra. The league always has to be your priority. To prove you are the best team over nearly 40 games is what you are judged by and what gives you the most satisfaction. But there are a number of 'extras' that are pretty important too. Top of the tree is playing for your country in a major tournament. After that, the next thing you want is to play in the Champions League or UEFA Cup. This season we were determined not to throw that privilege away.

The first game went as close to plan as you could wish for. We beat Helsinki 2–0 and I managed to get both goals. The first was a header from a cross by Lubo. The second came when Chris turned brilliantly on the edge of the box and played me in. I was able to get to the ball and dink it past their keeper as he tried to close me down.

Of course, we didn't think the tie was sewn up, but we were happy with the performance and we'd done all the things you are meant to do in a home leg. We travelled to the second leg feeling reasonably confident, but there were factors waiting to trip us up. Helsinki was very, very cold and the pitch was in poor condition. The stadium was small and that allowed the wind to blow across the ground. And then we went two goals down.

It wasn't that we were playing particularly badly, in fact we were playing quite well and, had a bit of luck come our way, we could probably have killed the tie off in the first half. I had chances to score, but I just couldn't find the net. It was one of those games.

When their second goal went in, my heart sank. I had really wanted us to make an impression in Europe, and to have been 2–0 up and then thrown it away was a real blow. We'd been pretty good so far at dealing with set-backs; if we conceded a goal, we simply knuckled down and tried to get one back. But, for a moment, I wondered if we were going to be able to do it this time. We were facing the possibility of going out of Europe and we were going to have to dig deep.

Collectively we decided enough was enough and set about retrieving the advantage we'd earned in the first leg. All we needed was one goal, and in extra time Chris managed to score it, to send our travelling support home happy. There were a few smiles in the changing room, but mostly out of a sense of relief. I remember thinking how easy it is to crash out of a cup. Not only do you need to play well, but you need the run of the ball. The more you play football, the more you realize there is a part of it that you cannot control. It's the part that makes a referee say the ball wasn't over the line when you know it was, or that means that on one day your passes are ending up in the crowd.

It's the same with scoring goals. As a striker, all I can do to tip the balance of luck in my favour is to train hard and work on the things that I'm going to need in the game.

One thing I know for sure is that you can't survive on talent alone. I did that up until I was 13, because I had some skills that the other kids didn't have. Then, because I was small for my age, I had to work on the other parts of my game, my strength, my fitness and my mind. Being able to anticipate what might happen, and to react quicker than opponents is a real advantage.

The sort of training we have been doing this season has been perfect for me in that respect. Because we play a lot of games in training and always work with the ball, I find you can stay sharp and keep your touch well-tuned. We generally split up into three zones and have a small game of one, two or three touch in each, depending on the zone. We then rest and start again. Because you are always moving and there are a lot of short bursts, it is similar to a game and also helps to keep down the amount of plain running you have to do.

One thing I don't practise much during the season is dead ball situations such as free-kicks. If you want to work on stuff like that, you have to stay after training, which is fine, but when you are playing two or three matches a week and training in between, it would probably do more harm than good to do that extra work. You do need to rest, because all those games tend to make your body break down a bit. And when the weather is cold and windy, the last thing you want to be doing is standing around, taking endless free-kicks. You'd probably end up with stiff and strained muscles. Perhaps, if I did practise free-kicks, I would get more on target, but then it might mean I wasn't as sharp in another part of my game. It's something I will work on a bit more in the summer.

The extra-time win against Helsinki set us up for a clash with the French cup holders, Girondins de Bordeaux, complete with players of the quality of French international, Christophe Dugarry. We were away in the first leg, which is okay because it leaves you knowing what you have to do at home. I wouldn't say we were exactly confident when we flew down the day before the game, but there was a good feeling, we knew what we were capable of. That evening we did a bit of light training before going for a meal. There was an air of anticipation among the players, knowing this was a big test. We were all aware that we were going to face a very strong team. French football has always been good, but since the national team won both the World Cup and the European Championship, playing their club sides has become more daunting.

Inside the stadium there was a lot of noise from the home fans, but I don't speak a word of French, so I have no idea what they were saying. I always figure that if supporters pay their money to go and watch a game, they have the right to give the opposition a bit of stick, as long as it's within reason. But there's a difference between the normal, good-natured abuse you expect and racist chants, or singling out players for attack. As always, the Celtic support wasn't going to be outdone and we could hear them clearly from their section of the ground.

I think we played some of our best football of the season that night. Chris had injured his ankle, so I was playing as a lone striker, with Lubo just behind me. We were perhaps a little defensive in the first 20 minutes or so, but, as the game started to open up, we began pushing forward and gave ourselves more room to play in. We were playing some very intelligent football, keeping possession, defending in depth and trying to catch them on the break. I had an early chance, but my header flew over the bar. There must have been only about a minute on the clock and I was mentally still back in the changing room, screwing my studs in, when Bobby sent the cross over. I got a slight knock in the face, which brought me to my senses, and a little while later I got past the defence, but my shot was weak and easy for the keeper. Nevertheless, I was getting into good positions and getting chances, and I felt the goal was going to come. So you can imagine what a blow it was to go a goal down.

The ball was swung over and we just didn't defend it properly. Our defence had been magnificent all season, but for a moment we lost concentration and got punished. Yet we still felt we could get something out of the game. We were playing well and weren't about to panic. A few minutes after they'd scored, the ball was played into the Bordeaux penalty area and one of their players tried to bring it under control. He slightly hesitated in clearing it and pushed it a bit far ahead of himself, allowing me to run around him and nick it away. He swung his boot and caught my legs.

That is what I mean by thinking quickly. The sort of games we were playing in training meant we were always aware of pouncing on the slightest mistake an opponent made. You know in a situation like that in the box that the defender is going to be under pressure and, if he can't get the ball, he might bring you down.

Having won the penalty, it was also my job to take it. I don't think I've ever taken a penalty and not been nervous. You know it's a great opportunity and, in a game like Bordeaux, it's possibly the chance to put you through to the next round. I normally decide on one corner as I'm placing the ball. I might change my mind immediately, but after that, it's fixed. I don't have any tricks, I just try to hit the ball cleanly and with power, so the keeper has the least amount of time to get to it.

I took a quick look at the keeper and then lashed the ball past him. Job done. It was good to go in at half-time on level terms. We stepped things up again in the second half, determined to hang on to the advantage that the away goal had given us. We played about six minutes of injury time, which seemed to last an eternity, as Bordeaux pressed for a winner and we were forced to defend desperately on a couple of occasions. It is amazing the amount of time that gets added on these days. Sometimes you hear the crowd trying to get the ref to blow for full-time and you feel tempted to join in the chorus of whistles.

Finally the referee decided that we had played for long enough, and we knew we'd earned a great result. I would have settled for that scoreline before the game and it was a plane full of contented footballers that headed out into the night sky and north. We were tired and I napped most of the way, occasionally running the penalty over in my mind.

A good result, yes, but far from a decisive one, and we weren't in any way complacent. I've played too many games in Europe to know that, unless you are 6–0 up from the first leg, the opposition are still in with a chance. But we knew we had one foot in the next round, and it wasn't just because we had come away with the draw. We had matched pretty much everything that Bordeaux had had to throw at us and we knew that, if we could do it again, we were within striking distance of the third round.

I suppose I wanted it particularly badly because it had been in the UEFA Cup that I'd been injured the year before. I felt I had been robbed of the chance to help Celtic progress and now I was being offered it again.

Back at Celtic Park, in front of a massive home crowd, a lot of people would have put money on us to go through. But that part of football you can't control was out in force that night. I think we played well. We certainly weren't playing defensively, but the fact was, as we knew when we kicked off at the start of the game, we were through, and if Bordeaux wanted to change that they were going to have to come and wrestle the game from us. We weren't going to throw everything forward and end up getting caught.

We did feel most of the real hard work had been done and when Lubo put us 1-0 up in the second half, the next round was beckoning. I don't think we relaxed or anything, there were just a few seconds when we didn't defend as well as we should have done, and that was it, they'd scored the equalizer. In football, as in most sports, fortunes can change in an instant. You can be on the opposition goal line one minute, and five seconds later you have conceded one yourself. Even in extra time we had chances. Stilian Petrov shot just wide and so did I. Perhaps we were snatching at the chances, I'm not sure. We still believed we would get the break.

After all, we'd played the best football, and the team that plays the best football wins, right? Wrong. Lillian Laslandes scored again for Bordeaux and that was that.

Losing that game was a real low point. There have been other more personal blows, but that was the most disappointing result on the pitch. At the end we virtually collapsed. For almost the first time in the season I felt really tired. We had played a good game and got caught with a couple of stupid goals. We felt we had let ourselves and the fans down. Back in the changing room, so often a place of laughter and joking in the previous months, everyone was pretty quiet. We knew we hadn't played badly, we'd just slipped up and been punished. Mr O'Neill knew we had tried, and failed because of a couple of mistakes. We'd only really made three mistakes over the two legs and conceded a goal on each occasion.

It was 9 November, one year and 19 days after I had broken my leg against a French club in the UEFA Cup. Now another French club had managed to spoil the party again and send my European dream packing for another year. I'll be looking to avoid the French next season.

chapter seven
into winter

Right from the moment Martin O'Neill took over at Celtic Park, he made it clear he would be looking to strengthen the squad, but only when quality players became available. A club like Celtic could have the biggest squad in football if it chose to, as there is no shortage of players who are desperate to become part of the Celtic experience, but there is no point in building up numbers just for the sake of it, and the manager was careful to go for players who he knew would fit into positions where he believed the team needed to be strengthened.

On 1 September, he signed Didier Agathe and Alan Thompson. I didn't know too much about Didier, except that he'd had some good games for Hibs. By the time he'd scored a great goal in the last minute to steal the points against Dundee on 10 December, I'd long since thought to myself, 'Yeah, we've bought ourselves quite some player here.'

Actually, when Didier first arrived, I thought he was a striker and it was only after a while that I realized he was a winger. His pace is incredible; he is probably the quickest player I have ever seen, quicker even than Marc Overmars. Didier's not just fast over the first 10 yards like some players, including me, but he just keeps on accelerating. I think he would be quite happy if they extended the length of the pitches, and then he might reach top speed after about 400 yards. At £35,000, he must be one of the best bargains ever. His contract was coming up for renewal and the manager took advantage of that. It was a very smart piece of business.

With the arrival of Didier, Mark Burchill was allowed to go out on loan to Birmingham. Obviously, Mark was unhappy that he was not getting the chance to play every week, and I can understand that. Players want to play, but players also come and go, and that's football.

Didier immediately struck me as a really laid-back character. He didn't say too much at first, but a lot of that was down to the fact that his English wasn't brilliant. When you have just arrived, it's tough to join in with a squad of players who are joking and speaking quickly particularly if you don't know the language very well. You miss a lot of things, especially the jokes – although that's not necessarily a bad thing. The important thing is to know the essentials. Most foreign footballers learn to swear first and then the usual calls on the pitch like 'man on'.

My English was always okay, although I could improve it if I studied hard. We learned English when I was at school in Sweden and we always heard a lot of English on records and TV. When I joined Feyenoord, I didn't speak any Dutch, but most people in Holland speak English, so for the first year-and-a-half I spoke nothing but English. It's not a problem.

Hopefully Jordan will grow up speaking both Swedish and English equally well, although it's often difficult to get him to speak in Swedish – he just says, 'No, speak English' – and he has a bit of a Scottish accent, says 'wee' for 'small', and if we're here for much longer, I'm sure he'll be saying, 'Nae bother.' I'm not sure that he realizes that he is Swedish at all.

I knew a bit more about Alan Thompson when he arrived, especially of his great left boot. Tommo's English was slightly better than Didier's and he immediately became a really lively presence around the club. Like Didier, he was also an instant success on the pitch. He can pass and go past people and he spots runs early and has a great awareness of what is going on around him. It was Tommo who set up our win on 23 September, against Dundee.

Dundee are a tough team and they battled for everything. They were well organized and it took a fantastic display from Johan Mjallby to keep them out. Around that time we were getting a bit of stick for grinding out results, but I think we played the sort of game that the situation demanded. If we got the chance, we always opened up and tried to play inventive football. But this is a tough league and everybody is after our scalp. If we had to, we were perfectly happy to stick our heels in and wear people down. The Dundee game was definitely one of those occasions, and I'm sure the manager and the fans were pleased with the result. It is only the press who get on your back if you're not playing 'champagne football' week in, week out.

We had some chances, but found it difficult to provide that all-important killer finish. Both Lubo and Joos had attempts scrambled away and I had a possible penalty turned down when I got sandwiched in the box. One of the first things you realize when you come to Scotland is that you can't cheat. I wouldn't anyway, but here I know that, if you were to pretend to go down, the chances are that you would be the one to get booked. To get a foul in Scotland, you have to be kicked. It's hard and physical and I admire that. I would much rather have it that way than the way it is in Italy or Spain, where players are always on the floor, the ref gives a free-kick and you lose the flow of the game.

It was about half an hour from the end that Tommo turned it for us. He put over a great cross and Stilian got on the end to bury it. Okay, it was a hard-fought victory, but I think we earned our pay that day.

Our next league match was on 10 October, away to Aberdeen, and it provided the papers with a major story. You see, we drew 1–1, not normally a result that would cause a huge amount of press coverage or discussion, but on this occasion it meant that we had dropped our first points of the season. Eight straight wins had racked us up 24 points. Of course, we never expected to go through the whole season with a 100 per cent record, but it was still a disappointment. When runs like that are going on, you don't think about them until they're over, and then it's too late to enjoy them.

It wasn't a good day for many reasons. We were a bit sluggish and never particularly looked like winners. Tommo had to go off in the first half with a hamstring strain and, in the second, Bobby Petta got sent off for two yellow cards. You could put our lack of invention down to the strain of playing every weekend and midweek, as we were at that time, but we shouldn't take anything away from Aberdeen, who played really well.

The upside was that we had fought back from a goal down, scored by Robbie Winters just before half-time. For me it was good to head the equalizer for two reasons. One, it was my 10th league goal of the season, and two, because I'd just had my dreadlocks cut off and there were loads of stories in the press along the lines of: 'Will Samson be so strong without his locks?'

It seems a bit silly, but I was conscious of wanting to score, just to show that cutting my hair off wouldn't have the slightest effect on my performance. When that ball shot off my head into the back of the net, I felt a sense of relief that had as much to do with me as it did with saving the point. And that's unusual.

It took a lot of willpower to cut off those dreads, believe me. I really felt I wanted a change, but I'd had my hair like that since I was 16 and it had sort of become my trademark, although I'd never intended it to. When I'd first done it as a teenager, I simply wanted a distinctive hairstyle, as a lot of kids do. It seemed fun and that was that. But over the years – and no pun intended here – you grow attached to a hairstyle. It was the way I looked when I met Magdalena and it's the way I look in our wedding pictures.

I'd actually thought about getting my hair cut the season before, and mentioned it to Magdalena, who had no objections. Then, when I broke my leg, there seemed to be a lot more important things to worry about than my hair, so I put it off.

It was one afternoon after training, a couple of days before the Aberdeen game, that I drove my car from the ground and, when I reached the London Road, I stopped. I normally take a left to go home to Bothwell, but right was the hairdressers. It's a good job that there were no cars behind me, because I sat there going, 'Left, no right, no left, er, right.' Then I just thought, 'Oh well', and swung the car towards the hairdressers.

I stormed in and said, 'Cut it all off!' We'd talked about it a few times, but I don't think they really believed I'd do it. Off it came and

I looked in the mirror expecting to feel totally different. But I didn't, I just looked a bit bald, quite distinguished in fact. 'Yeah, no problem,' I thought, 'but where's Henrik?'

Of course, I did feel a little bit guilty, since there were loads of people running around with Henrik Larsson masks complete with dreadlocks that were now a bit out of date. I don't think the shaven-headed version of the mask will ever really catch on. Those masks always made me smile. I think it's great when fans want to have a laugh. Football should be about fun and feeling you are all part of the same party.

I've been lucky, really lucky, with the Celtic fans. I'll always try to give autographs and stop for pictures, because I think it's flattering that people have taken the trouble to come along to the ground or wherever. Here in Scotland the fans are also a lot more understanding about your privacy. I have no problem at all with stopping for the supporters, but I always say my home and my family are not a part of that. I am, in a way, the property of the Celtic supporters while I'm at the ground, or training, but my home and my family is just for me. I want to keep that to myself, and the Celtic fans have always respected that.

It wasn't the case in Holland. You would get people turning up at your door for autographs. You would give them and then they'd be back wanting one for their brother, or friend, or whatever. Sometimes I'd have just got back from training and was trying to have a nap when they'd be knocking at the door. Thankfully, things are much better in Scotland.

Disappointing though it was, the loss of our 100 per cent record was put into stark perspective by the frightening illnesses of Morten

Wieghorst and Alan Stubbs. I was shocked and scared because we just didn't know what would happen next. These were people I worked with, had grown to know and had become friends with outside of football.

Morten had first started to feel unwell on the flight back from the Helsinki game, when it looked like he had the flu. On the following Monday, the day after we played Aberdeen, he was rushed to hospital and a few days later he was diagnosed with Guillain-Barré Syndrome, which is a rare brain virus. I was away with the Swedish international squad and I caught sight of something in the papers about Morten. I couldn't really work out what it was all about, so as soon as I was able to get back to the hotel I rang Magdalena, who knows all the people at the club, and the wives and girlfriends, and was keeping in touch with what was going on. She told me all about it and I remember feeling totally stunned – just cold and really scared for Morten. Obviously, I knew he would get great treatment but, when it is something that you don't feel you have any control over, it can be quite terrifying.

Then, about a month after that shock, we learned that Stubbsie was possibly going to have to face cancer again. It had showed up on a routine scan and the news rocked the club. If going out of the UEFA Cup was the lowest point in football terms, what happened to Morten and Stubbsie was the lowest point for everyone personally. It really took the wind out of us and a lot of the joy went out of what we were doing. Of course, we still wanted to win and keep on going. Moping around on the pitch wasn't going to help those guys. But, as soon as the game was over, we would think about them, and winning and losing became unimportant.

Despite the effect on our mood, we managed to keep playing the focused, versatile game we had been playing from the start of the season. After Aberdeen, we tucked three more wins under our belts, a 2–0 home win over St Mirren, 2–0 away to St Johnstone and 2–1 at home to Dundee United. There was an extraordinary sense of purpose amongst all of us, possibly strengthened by the determination to fight for Morten and Stubbsie. We wanted to win more than ever and we knew that a moment's loss of concentration could lead to a slip-up, and let the pursuing clubs back in the race.

The Scottish Premier League is a tough league to ply your trade in as a footballer. I've been defending this league almost since the day I arrived here and I'm starting to get tired of it. I'll say this now and I'll stick by it. This league is a great deal stronger than people want to give it credit for. It's not the strongest in the world, not the best, I won't claim that, but it's comparable with most of the other top European leagues. People say Celtic and Rangers dominate the SPL, but that's not true. Every week we meet sides that can give us a hard game. Okay, so Celtic and Rangers may be the big clubs that everyone wants to emulate, but that is the same everywhere. The English Premiership is meant to be one of the best leagues in Europe, but how many times in the last decade has it been won by Manchester United? In Spain it's usually Real Madrid or Barcelona who share the spoils, with the odd challenge from the likes of Valencia, and the Dutch League is dominated by PSV, Feyenoord and Ajax.

For those people who want to knock the SPL, I say come here and play in it, then make up your mind. The pace of the game is breathtaking, which was the first thing I noticed when I arrived from

Holland, and, although you get accustomed to it, it still seems quick. It is also a very physical league and you have to be strong to survive.

I could certainly have done with more of Chris Sutton's physical presence up front, where he could take some of the heat off me, but he had picked up a couple of injuries, to his ankle and a long-running toe problem, and Tommy Johnson had taken his place. Tommy is a fine footballer and did a great job for us, scoring some crucial goals just at the time when we most needed them towards the end of the season, but neither he nor I are target men in the sense that Chris is, so it did mean that some of our options were reduced and we had to adapt our game a bit. There was no point whacking the ball upfield for us to win.

At this point in the season the games were coming thick and fast. But playing matches is the good bit, so we weren't really complaining. We'd play at the weekend, warm down the next day, do some light training, play a midweek match, warm down, train, play the weekend, and on and on. If you keep playing and get a decent amount of rest, you don't feel too tired. Your legs recover between games and you can keep going. The trouble comes if you pick up a niggling injury because it doesn't get a chance to mend, and things that would normally clear up quickly can stay with you.

We travelled to Motherwell on 29 October, just three days after our tough UEFA Cup match in Bordeaux, and came away with a 3–3 draw from a hard game. Who knows how much that battling draw in Bordeaux had drained us, but we led twice and couldn't hang on to it. We had taken an early lead when Johan fired my pass into the roof of the net, before going behind 2–1. After battling back to 2–2, Johan knocked one in from an Alan

Thompson corner – only for the ref to say it was cleared before it went over the line. It was frustrating, but we weren't going to change his mind. We managed to go ahead again with about 20 minutes to play, when Jackie McNamara and I played a one-two and he fired home. But a few minutes later, Johan's bad luck struck again when he had a penalty awarded against him, and Motherwell equalized from the spot. Still, I regarded it as a point gained rather than two dropped.

A few days later we were on much better form to knock Hearts out of the CIS Cup in the fourth round, with a 5–2 win at Tynecastle. I was rested and some of the youngsters got another chance to shine. Stephen Crainey, Jamie Smith and Colin Healy were all among the scorers in a game that required extra time, having finished 2–2 after 90 minutes. Lubo and Jackie scored right at the end, but it was a great day for the young lads and showed what a strong youth programme there is at Celtic.

After that high, the rollercoaster hit another low four days later when Paul Lambert limped off at Kilmarnock with an ankle injury. It was a game we dominated, but Chris and I had a bad day in front of goal and were saved by Alan Thompson, who managed to get on the end of Didier's cross mid-way through the second half for the only goal of the game. But the joy of getting such a hard-fought victory was soured by the loss of Lambert.

His experience at Borussia Dortmund, where he won the European Cup in 1998, has given him an ability to play great, intelligent football. He gets up for balls others wouldn't reach, he tackles, turns players and is a real inspiration. He had been a driving force in our midfield, and players like that are very hard to replace.

Fortunately, the boss had managed to sign Neil Lennon, who immediately proved to be another astute purchase with a great début when we beat Dundee 2–1. He has a lot of international experience and you could see right away what a cool head he has in the middle of the park. Like Lambert, he's a composed midfield player who is good in the tackle and can pass. Added to which, he's a really nice guy and he immediately settled in, both on and off the pitch.

In the next games we disposed of St Johnstone 4–1 and had a great 6–1 win over Hearts. I managed to get two goals in each game, taking my league tally to 17, and the win over Hearts also meant we opened up an eight-point lead over Hibs, who lost 2–0 to Aberdeen. Of equal significance, we had a fifteen-point lead over Rangers.

One of the main planks of our success so far in the season had been a solid defence. The back four have something like 200 international caps between them and that is the sort of experience that pays off under constant pressure, as we were facing week after week in the SPL, where every game can seem like a cup final. As a forward, it is a real comfort to know that we have those guys at the back, that the security is there if you go and do something stupid. You know that even a potentially dangerous situation at the back can be cleared up and turned into an attack of our own. The simple fact was we were not conceding many goals.

To go down 5–1 to Rangers at Ibrox was both a shock and a disappointment. They scored 10 minutes before half-time and I equalized 10 minutes into the second half, but after that we just fell apart. It's not nice to lose, and it's definitely not nice to lose to Rangers by that sort of score. After the way we had been playing, and considering the fact we had thrashed them 6–2 a short while before, the result was unexpected I suppose, but in a game like that, with those sorts of pressures, it is often essential to score first.

I think that result showed two things. Firstly, how unpredictable the Old Firm match is, and secondly, that you are inevitably going to lose some games, and the important thing is to bounce straight back. I know for the Celtic supporters crammed into Ibrox, it must have seemed like a terrible ordeal. They had had just three months to enjoy our 6–2 triumph, and now it was Rangers' turn to gloat. That hurt the players too, but you have to put it into perspective and remember it is just one game. In the same way that our victory over Rangers didn't win us the championship, so the defeat didn't lose it for us either. That is more or less what the manager said afterwards. You know you have to keep your head up and go out and make amends the next weekend. Of course, we were a little stunned at the end of it, and probably a little embarrassed to have let in five goals, but there was a determination to make sure that, at the end of the season, it would mean very little.

I'd love to say that we bounced back the following week with a great victory, but it's too easy to check the records and see that a trip to Hibs on a windy day ended 0–0. We desperately wanted to bury the memory of the previous week, but, again, we didn't get the luck.

However, with the winter break looming, we were determined to finish the first part of the season on a high. The last thing we wanted was to spend the break knowing we had not done ourselves justice. And a run of six wins in a row, beating Dunfermline, Dundee, Aberdeen, St Mirren, Dundee United and Kilmarnock, scoring 23 goals and conceding just two, meant we had no worries on that score.

After the Rangers and Hibs away games, it was nice to get back to the Park to face Dunfermline. Whether it was because we were at home or not, I don't know, but we turned on a great display in the first half to go in 2–1 up, after falling behind with just a minute gone. A late goal by Tommy Johnson clinched it, and our roll began.

Early in December the manager brought in Ramon Vega from Tottenham, to strengthen the centre of the defence at a time when injuries were starting to leave us a little thin on the ground. He had the dream debut, scoring twice in the 6–0 win over Aberdeen.

I managed to score 10 goals in those six games before the break, including four against Kilmarnock, and I felt great. I've sometimes heard the expression 'scoring for fun', and although scoring is always fun, I knew what it meant during that run. It just doesn't seem to matter how you hit the ball, it is going to go in. And the more you score, the less you think about it, so the more relaxed you are, and the easier it all becomes. Added to which, I was getting excellent service and delivery from the rest of the team. It all works in this cycle. You score and build confidence, so you try more things, your teammates have confidence in you, so they keep getting the ball to you and then luck decides to come onto your side for a while.

I suppose that, if there is any secret to scoring goals it is knowing where to be at the right time. You have to be there to score. Anticipation comes with playing a lot of football and knowing how your teammates play. I don't think defenders who play against Celtic ever think, 'I want to stop Henrik Larsson.' I'm sure they are just thinking that they want to stop Celtic. They know that, if they concentrate on me, there are plenty of other players who can punish them.

That last match before the winter break, against Kilmarnock, has to have been one of the best I played in all season. It was just after the New Year, and before the match there was absolute silence from the 60,000 packed inside the Park in honour of the victims of the Ibrox disaster in 1971. As soon as the tribute ended, the roof was lifted by a roar from the fans and I could feel a tingle go down the back of my neck. It was a day for giving your all.

We started well, playing some neat football, but initially the Kilmarnock defence held firm. There was just the slightest feeling of frustration creeping in as we let a few chances go begging, including a free-kick that I hit wide from 20 yards. Then Chris, back from injury, scored shortly before half-time to send us in with a bit of relief.

The second half was a completely different story. After about 55 minutes, Stilian Petrov got the ball from Chris and appeared to be fouled. Everyone stopped, expecting the whistle, but when none came I slipped through the defence and put the ball over the keeper. It was another of those moments when you need to be aware of what is going on around you and act quickly. Chris scored again a few minutes later and, with about 20 minutes to go, I headed home a cross from Stilian. Three minutes after that, I scored the 100th goal of my Celtic career, thanks to a great pass by Alan Thompson. It was fantastic to hear the crowd really behind us, and, when Lubo put over another low cross, I managed to get my boot on the end of it to steer it into the net.

My total for the season now stood at 32 – 28 of them scored in the league – and I was in the perfect frame of mind to enjoy the winter break.

chapter eight
the break

Christmas in the Larsson house that year was a lot of fun. Celtic had played St Mirren away on 23 December, and the next day is when Swedish people celebrate Christmas and give presents – but not until the evening, which is pretty tough when you are a kid.

We always have a lunch of ham and sausages, meatballs and vegetables. We also eat porridge and fish – but not at the same time. As with most homes around the country, and probably around the world, TV plays a big part in Christmas entertainment. In Sweden there is a Disney cartoon programme every afternoon during Christmas, and that's the time to sit around and take it easy, as cartoons are one of the things that keep Jordan quiet.

Of course, with games on throughout the Christmas holidays, you can't go too far with your celebrations, but that's okay. While the rest of the world is feeling stuffed and can't move, footballers feel fine. The club holds a big Christmas dinner for everyone and their families, which is always a lot of fun. And there are all sorts of events organized for us at places like The Thistle or the Glasgow Hilton.

I'm a big supporter of the winter break. It's not that I don't like playing in the cold – I'm from Sweden, so I know what it's like to play in freezing conditions, and when I made my debut for Feyenoord against Vitesse, it was minus six degrees and the pitch was frozen solid. But there are times when pitches are totally unplayable and dangerous. Even after the winter break, some games are called off, so the chances are it will be a real lottery for those few weeks. I'm sure supporters don't want to see games played on terrible pitches, or travel miles to a game to have it called off at the last minute. I also think the winter break helps everybody to recharge. Players come back from it eager to play and the supporters eager to watch.

Of course, this year we knew we could go away and relax, with a nice cushion between us and Hibs. The plan was that we would all have a week off and not think about football at all, and then the squad would meet up at our training camp in Florida. It seemed like a good idea to take the family to Orlando, where we could have a good holiday and wouldn't have far to go to meet up with the squad afterwards. When you have a small child, travelling anywhere can be like a military exercise and the less you do of it, the better.

Myself, Magdalena and Jordan went with Tommy Johnson, Alan Thompson and Chris Sutton and their families. It is one of the pleasures of club football when the people you work with become friends. If you are close to each other off the field, it helps you to bond on the field, particularly when the going gets tough.

Being at Celtic is like having a huge family. We all see each other every day at work, we share jokes, injuries, successes, failures and worries. We have dinner at each others' houses and play golf together. The boys are always arranging 'outings', such as go-karting. It is like a soap opera in many ways.

Orlando proved to be the perfect place to go to, although the weather was a bit of a surprise. Leaving the icy conditions of

Glasgow, we were looking forward to getting a bit of sun, but when we arrived in Florida, known as 'The Sunshine State', it was cold and rainy. We couldn't believe it. Of course, the children didn't care. It was just the adults who had frowns on their faces. We went to the Universal Studios, Disney World and Sea World. Apparently most people who go to Sea World get wet because the killer whale splashes them, we got wet because it rained constantly. But it was a load of fun and the grown-ups became kids again.

The SPL seemed a million miles away and all the tension and pressure of professional football was put to one side for a few days of fun. It's not until you stop doing something that you realize how much of your life is taken up by it. I love playing football and I love playing for Celtic, but it's nice when you can stand back from it, and that's what stops it consuming your whole life. It hasn't really happened to me yet, that football has ever seemed like a chore, and I would hate for it to ever get like that.

At the end of the week the rest of the team turned up and it was back to work – sort of. We were all staying at the Marriott World Centre, which is a huge hotel used a lot by businessmen. It has everything you could want to help relax and keep fit – there are saunas and pools and a golf course, which got a fair bit of use. For someone who enjoys a round of golf as much as I do, it was ironic that I had been living and working in the home of golf and had rarely had the opportunity to play in recent months. We were playing so much football that I had to travel thousands of miles to get a round in.

I first started playing golf with friends in Sweden years ago. We weren't very good and just played on the public courses. At that time I would never have thought about going to any of the big private clubs where the rich people played. I had only one set of clubs and took them to Holland when I joined Feyenoord. I just played five or six times then, but it was still something I loved doing. The minute you stand on the first tee and hit the ball, you don't think about anything else. It is the best escape there is. Of course, moving to Scotland was ideal. Some of the very best courses in the world can be found there and I've managed to play most of them. In fact, I'll play wherever they let me.

I managed to get my handicap down to 13 before I broke my leg – perhaps that's what brought the bad luck. It's back down to 14 now and maybe I'll try to skip 13 and go straight to 12.

One of my favourite places in the world is Gleneagles. The course is superb and the hotel is just fantastic. It's one of the places Magdalena and I go when we have a couple of days free. We take Jordan up and even Simba gets to go. There can't be many places in the world where you are better looked after.

While we were in Florida, we organized a golf tournament and although I couldn't hit the side of a barn door that day, we had a great time. It was mostly organized for the Celtic supporters' clubs out there and everyone joined in. Young Stephen Crainey won it and joint second were Jamie 'Smudger' Smith and Colin Healy. The young lads are not only promising footballers, but they can put a few of us old hands to shame around the golf course as well.

The youth programme looks good for Celtic's future at the moment, and while there are a number of fine players arriving on the fringe of the first team, the three mentioned above are the pick of the crop at the moment, along with Shaun Maloney. Smudger and Colin Healy are both good strikers of the ball, with a lot of skill and the ability to go past defenders. Stephen Crainey is a very promising young defender with a cool head. He is also good going forward, with a very sweet left foot and a great shot. Shaun is another forward with a lot of skill. The first time I saw him on the pitch, I remember thinking, 'Wow! There's not much wrong with this guy.' He's not the biggest lad, but that's something I can relate to, and he does seem very strong. He scored 22 goals in 24 starts with the youth team and you can't knock that sort of record. It's good having them around with us, and if they ever need advice there are always players they can ask.

I remember when I was a young player, I thought I knew most things and didn't particularly want advice. But as you grow up you realize that you don't know everything and that you can always learn something new. At the grand old age of 29, when I'm normally one of the senior players, both at Celtic and in the Swedish team, I still find I'm learning. Situations often come up in games that I haven't encountered before. I think the young Celtic lads are going about things the right way: they watch what the older players are doing and do talk about football with them. Then they turn it on when they get the chance to play.

In Florida we had a couple of little practice games in which the young guys took part, and did well. You always hope you can play well and help them learn a few things, but you never think you want to get one over on them, or take the Mickey out of them on the pitch. If Stephen Crainey tackles me and gets the ball, well done to him.

We trained at the Disney sports ground and, although we might have had a few laughs at the name when we found out, that stopped pretty soon after we got there. It was immaculate, the pitches were like putting greens and perfect for passing. It was great playing on a surface like that.

The idea of the training camp is mostly to stay fit and work on a few things, keep the team spirit up and relax. The weather got much better, and as we heard the temperatures had fallen to about minus eight in Glasgow, the sun was beating down. It was great to see Morten lying by the pool, taking in the sun, starting to look a lot fitter and healthier. He'd finally come out of Southern General hospital mid-way through December, much to the relief of everyone at the club. Around the same time we learned that Stubbsie was doing well and would be having an operation in January, about which the doctors were very confident.

Paul Lambert was also taking a full part in training and fighting back to fitness. His dislocated ankle and damaged ligaments were not giving him any trouble, and it was reassuring for the rest of us to know that there was a good chance of him being back in the side that was going to take on Stranraer in the cup, once we were back from the break.

There were a couple of dinners organized by the Celtic supporters' clubs in Florida, whose commitment always bowls me over when we travel. Everywhere we go there are Celtic fans. It didn't take me long after I'd arrived in Scotland to get an idea of how big Celtic is, but it's only when you go all over the world and meet the green and white hoards that it really sinks in.

The American fans were great, they were fanatical in the best sense of the word. It's incredible that people who rarely get the chance to travel to games love the club so much. Some of the guys were presented with awards at the dinners and it was touching to sit next to them and chat about football, and realize how much it meant to them that Celtic had come over to see them. A few thousand miles and the Atlantic Ocean were not nearly enough to dampen their enthusiasm for the club.

The big event was a dinner at the Marriott ballroom, organized by John Howley, president of the Orlando Celtic Supporters' Club. There were endless photographs and autograph signings, and some really moving speeches from local supporters. They talked of great times gone by and of the great future that they see for the club. For a relative newcomer like me, it felt an honour to be a part of all this. Bobby and Johan got the OSCS's Player of the Year awards and Alan Stubbs and Morten Wieghorst won awards for the spirit they have shown in adversity.

The manager gave a great speech, with a few digs at Alan Thompson, which had everyone in fits of laughter. It was obvious that the American fans thought a great deal of Martin O'Neill. The final award of the night went to John Clark, our kit man and member of the famous Lisbon Lions, for all his hard work over the years.

Martin O'Neill and I were also presented with awards from the SPL for being manager and player of the month. It's lovely to get awards like that, but you always know that it is a reflection of the guys around you.

The day after the big dinner, we had our first competitive match, against the University of South Florida in Tampa. Unfortunately the ground didn't come anywhere close to resembling the condition of the training ground. To say it was terrible would be doing it a favour. I think it had been used for all sorts of different sports and there was hardly any grass at all. Football, or soccer in these parts, obviously doesn't come very high on the list of priorities.

I can't remember exactly why, but I was given the number 22 shirt to wear while Didier took my usual number seven. I was given the number seven shirt when I first moved to Celtic, and now I'm pretty attached to it. You get like that about your shirt. Not only is it easy for people to identify you with a number, but it almost becomes a lucky charm as well. I played 17 at Helsingborg, and then changed to 10.

For some reason I've never liked the idea of wearing a number nine, and, if I don't get seven, I want some high number. Having said all that, I don't want to sound like it's something that I worry about too much. It isn't. Probably the younger lads care more than us old ones about the numbers. But I like seven.

Obviously my shirt has a good effect, because Didier had a magnificent match. He ran the ball all over the pitch and sprayed some great passes. Alan Thompson scored a couple and, despite the surface, there were some good performances. We had a great sing-song on the way back that night and everyone was in good spirits. The work and play were nicely mixed and most evenings we got time off to do whatever we wanted. The group of us who came to Orlando early had picked out a few nice restaurants and we headed back with our wives a couple of times.

One night we all took in a basketball match between the Chicago Bulls and Orlando Magic, which was a great occasion. I'm not sure football will ever gain the razzmatazz of American sport – I'm not sure the cheerleaders could really cope with dancing in December in Dundee. But it's great in the right place, and at a basketball match it adds to a brilliant atmosphere. Having said that, I'm sure the crowd at Orlando's stadium would be overwhelmed by the atmosphere at Celtic Park when we're entertaining Rangers. I've liked basketball for a long time and used to play a little bit of one-on-one in the street. I named Jordan after the great Chicago basketball star Michael Jordan. I admired his determination and spirit.

The second game of the mini-tour was against an American professional side, Tampa Bay Mutiny. I'm not sure exactly why football has never become very big in the US. It's had some great players, and still does. There is now quite a bit of home grown talent – the likes of Claudio Reyna for instance – and some big foreign names. It's had to compete with long-established American sports, but it does appear that more and more young Americans are taking to football.

I was lucky enough to play in the World Cup in the US in 1994, when the crowds were really good, and it felt like football might be going somewhere. That summer remains one of the highlights of my career, even though I probably let myself down a little by not making the initial starting line-up. I'd turned up for training camp feeling really tired and my touch just wasn't there.

I was on the bench for the first match against Cameroon. With about 25 minutes left, we were 2–1 down and the coach told me I was going on. It's an amazing moment making your debut in a World Cup Finals. I hadn't been on long when I got the ball just outside the centre circle and had a mad idea to shoot. I hit it with everything I had and watched as it bounced back off the crossbar and Martin Dahlin scored the rebound.

The following game I had a stinker against Brazil, while playing on the left wing. It's not a position I like too much, but I think the bigger problem was that I gave Brazil too much respect. There are some teams that have half a goal before they leave the dressing room, and Brazil is one of them. We managed to draw 1–1, but my performance meant I was back on the bench for the next game against Russia, which we won 3–1. To be honest, it was a swelteringly hot day and it wasn't too much of an effort to sit it out in the air-conditioned dug-out.

Following a 3–1 win over Saudi Arabia, we threw away a 1–0 lead in the last 10 minutes against Romania in the quarter-final. With the score standing at 2–2 after extra time, the game went to penalties. I was nominated to take the sixth penalty and, as the first players stepped up to the spot, I remember sitting on the grass praying that I wouldn't have to take one. I've always had to take penalties and think I'm okay when it comes to spot kicks – I've done it so often I know the places you need to aim for and the sort of pace you need to put on the ball – but that doesn't mean it isn't nerve-wracking, and when it can mean the difference between going through to the semi-final of the World Cup or not, you can multiply that a few times.

I'd been sitting in the centre circle thinking about the penalties I'd taken right from being a kid, and trying to calm myself down. Both sides missed their first efforts and then matched each other for the remaining four. So it came to me. I hit it right, the keeper went left and the ball sneaked in off a post. At the time I felt a huge sense of happiness and relief, but even now I flinch when I see it. A few more inches, in an effort to get it as far from the keeper as possible, and it would have bounced back.

We lost to Brazil in the semi-final and so ended up in the third/fourth place play-off against Bulgaria. We won 4–1, and I walked the ball round the keeper to score. That goal will certainly be one of the ones that I'll be re-telling to my grandchildren as I sit in my rocking chair.

Unfortunately, the performance against Tampa didn't exactly match my previous experiences in the States. Yet again, the fans were incredible. There was only really one proper stand in the ground and it was again filled with a sea of green and white. They were singing before, during and after the game, and it's just a shame that we didn't play the sort of football that matched the occasion. To be fair, no-one wanted to risk picking up an injury, and I think we were holding back a bit. Tampa were a very competitive side, built around the Colombian star Carlos Valderrama in midfield. I sat out the second half as we made countless substitutions, and although Didier Agathe and Tommy Johnson went close near the end, 2–1 was a fair result.

Saying goodbye to Florida was quite tough. We'd had a great time. It had been the sort of break we needed, and the hospitality of everybody there had made a real impression on all of us.

Our last job before going back to Scotland was a quick diversion to Norwich to play in a testimonial match for City's long-serving physio Tim Sheppard. Footballers never mind playing in games like that because you know there are these people behind the scenes who do so much and never get into the spotlight. I know how much I owe to Brian Scott at Celtic.

Around 6,000 Celtic fans made the eight-hour journey to Norwich, and we gave them something to sing about with a 4–2 win. I scored with a volley into the top corner from Jackie McNamara's throw-in, but it was no easy ride. The temperature was absolutely freezing, and something of a shock after flying in from Florida. Bobby Petta used to play for Norwich, so he got a bit of stick from the local fans, and it was quite a physical match, as you would expect from a tough Nationwide League side. As preparation for playing in a British league again, it was a bit like a diver going into a decompression chamber on his way back to the surface. At the end, both sets of fans gave a great reception to the players and Mr O'Neill was greeted with cheers by as many Norwich fans as Celtic supporters.

And so back home. Of course, it's impossible to say what the best use of the winter break is. If you go away and then everything goes well afterwards, you think that the secret is going away. If we had come back and lost six in a row, we would probably be told we'd wasted the time. What happens at the end of the season sort of dictates how wisely you have used the winter break. But I think, however you spend it, the break is a good idea.

Still, it was nice to get back home, put my feet up in front of the TV and watch Jordan race around the house, finding all his toys again and generally making as much noise as is possible for a three-and-a-half-year-old to make.

chapter nine
welcome back

Reality sometimes has a habit of landing on your doorstep with a crash. The Florida fun and the daily diet of golf, swimming, training on bowling green flat pitches in 20 degrees centigrade, and friendly football matches, definitely seemed like a dream when we stepped out at Stranraer for the Scottish Cup third round on 28 January.

It was cold, the surface was far from perfect and Sky TV had sent their cameras to the ground, no doubt hoping for another Inverness Caledonian Thistle.

I'm sure the Celtic side that faced Inverness never thought for a moment that they would slip up so badly, but it may have been that they just lost concentration for a moment, and you simply can't do that. If there is one big difference between the present Celtic team and others I have played in since arriving in Scotland, it is our toughness, organisation and, it has to be said, confidence. You don't ever underestimate your opponent, but you have to believe in yourselves. And we do.

Stranraer started with determination, but I think we never really looked like giving anything away. It was good that our defence was on top form – we'd gone four games without conceding a goal – because up front we were letting a few opportunities slip.

Didier put a great cross on my head in the first few minutes, only for the Stranraer keeper, Mark McGeown, to tip it away. From the corner, Ramon Vega had a good chance, but fired over. And then I hit one wide. It's pretty frustrating when you're not putting them away, but at least we were creating opportunities and that is the important thing.

The breakthrough finally came when Joos Valgaeren scored with a far-post header and got a kick in the face for his troubles. Although Stranraer kept battling, we never looked like giving up the lead, and added goals by Jackie McNamara – a good effort from 15 yards out, and Lubo Moravcik right at the end, in addition to an own goal. Stranraer pulled one back in the last 10 minutes, but it meant little. It was good to get that game out of the way and show anyone who had any doubts that we were a more determined unit this year.

On paper, the next game, away to Hearts in the SPL, should have been a much harder match. It was tough, but the hardest thing about it was the pitch. The weather had become even colder and the referee came close to calling it off. In the end he declared it playable and we had to get on with it. Hearts' undersoil heating saved the ground from icing up completely, but it could do nothing to keep us warm. In the second half it started snowing and I remember looking at the small flakes drifting down from the steel blue sky and thinking that this was no weather in which to be playing football.

Some players like to wear gloves or layers of shirts when it's cold, but not me. No matter how cold it is, once you start running around you are going to warm up and then what you don't want is loads of clothes on because you start getting sweaty. There is nothing worse than sweating on a freezing day, because, as soon as you stop, the sweat starts to cool down and you end up getting really chilled. I might just wear a T-shirt under my football shirt to start off with, but I'll take it off as soon as I start to warm up.

In Sweden we have a winter build-up and I've learned over the years how to play in those sorts of conditions. You know that it's going to be slippery and that the ball is going to skid off the surface, so you don't want to overhit passes and you don't want to be running so fast that you can't stop.

My Swedish winter training paid off because I got a hat-trick in a 3–0 win, to take my league total past the 30 mark. The first came inside five minutes, when Alan Thompson delivered a great free-kick and I got my head to it at the far post. The second was another great ball from Tommo on the left wing, which he whipped into the box with such pace that I only had to flick it with the outside of my right boot to divert it into the left side of the net, past the keeper's dive.

About 10 minutes from time, I got the ball in the centre circle, pushed it past one defender and then found Didier Agathe on the left. Because Didier is so quick, I knew I could put a little extra on the ball to keep it away from the defence and he would still be able to reach it. Didier made good ground on the left and passed back into the area. I took it first on the chest, then cushioned it on my thigh and volleyed it home. It looked good, but I wasn't trying to appear flash, it was just the right way to score at the time. I couldn't get my head to Didier's cross and there was no way I could have volleyed it first time, so I had to take it down. The way you train with the ball gives you the confidence to do things in matches, but some of it is also instinct, an instinct that simply tells you to do something in a particular way.

I think I had some skills when I was a kid that the other boys didn't have. I would practise doing things that I'd developed as I still do now. I was always pushing the ball past people, or trying to drag it back with my sole, and, like a lot of young lads, I used to practise keeping the ball in the air. But I wasn't doing half the tricks with the ball that you see youngsters doing now. Seriously, some of the things I see today's young players do just leave me speechless, I wouldn't have known how to start doing those things when I was a kid.

The Hearts game was pretty physical and Joos was an early victim when he went off in the first few minutes with a badly injured ankle. I hate seeing a teammate go down in pain, especially as, since my injury, I always fear the worst. Fortunately, it turned out to be ligament strains rather than the fracture they suspected at first, but it was another blow to lose Joos, who had been inspirational all season. His size and pace are a great asset when you are trying to turn defence into attack. It was lucky that we had recently bought Ramon Vega, who could play in that role and was already proving a strong competitor.

The Hearts match was the first game in which we truly saw the Lennon and Lambert partnership in central midfield, with Paul totally recovered from his ankle injury. Some people had voiced doubts about whether the two would work together, but if you have quality players you play them and they adapt. Even though they are both defensive midfield players, they do like to come forward and they soon showed the creative side to their game. They were also helped by being given clearly defined roles, which is one of the great things about our coaching team – they always send us out with a clear understanding of what our job is in each game.

With his own chances of earning a regular place in midfield looking bleak, Eyal Berkovic left to go on loan to Blackburn. He was one of several good players who weren't getting as much first team action as they would have liked, because of the strength of the squad, and he felt it important to go somewhere where he would get regular games. When Eyal had played, he had played well, especially in his performance against Jeunesse. He has a lot of skill and I always liked the way he spotted runs early. But the simple fact was that we had other players in his position who were gelling perfectly. In freezing conditions, Neil and Paul dominated against Hearts and we showed creativity throughout the side. It was exactly the sort of match you wanted to have under your belt when approaching a double header against Rangers.

We were to face them in the CIS Cup semi-final and then again a few days later in a crucial SPL match. I would be lying if I said we paid no attention to Rangers, or that we didn't bother looking out for their results, but the fact is, it isn't something we ever make much of a deal out of. We are always aware of Rangers, they are our arch-rivals, and when this season started we knew they were the side we would have to finish above to win the league. But you can easily slip up if you are paying too much attention to one side. We have tried to simply concentrate on ourselves this season.

It's fine if Rangers, or Hibs, are dropping points, but it is much more important that we are also getting good results ourselves.

Quite often you get an indication if Rangers have gone behind by the roar that goes through the Celtic fans. The first time I witnessed that I was really confused. I can't remember who we were up against, but I know that nothing much was happening on the pitch and suddenly there was this ripple of noise around the ground, which quickly became a big cheer. 'What's all that about?' I asked, a little bemused. Tom Boyd smiled at me and said, 'I think that's Rangers going a goal behind.'

And so we headed into one of the biggest weeks of the season for Glasgow football. We approached the first game, the semi-final, like it was the most important game in the world. That's the only way that you can do it, in my book. There was no point playing that game with one eye on the league match a few days later. I remember waking up in the hotel on the morning of the first game and having a moment's pause before realizing what the day was. Suddenly there is a little flip in your stomach and you're out of bed. I don't think it's nerves, so much as excitement. You desperately want to get out on the Park and put an end to the days of hype.

We got off to a great start when Chris Sutton scored in the first five minutes, following up when Ramon's header rebounded off the crossbar. About 10 minutes later a long ball from Johan Mjallby was picked up by Robert Malcom, but he seemed to lose control momentarily and that let me sneak in to take it off him. As Stephan Klos came out of his goal, I lobbed it over him to double the lead.

I think getting the two-goal cushion led us into committing the cardinal sin of sitting back a bit and we let Rangers back into the game. Suddenly we found the momentum was with them. When you have the bit between your teeth, you find the ball keeps breaking to your side and the opposition start getting rattled. Just before half time, after quite a bit of Rangers' possession, we conceded a penalty. They scored, the tension increased and the game became pretty heated. Cards were handed out all over the place. I wasn't counting, but I think I avoided getting one. Obviously Rangers were desperate to get back into the game and we were desperate to hold on and push for another goal. Inevitably it became physical. With about 20 minutes left, I scored again and, soon after, I was substituted for Lubo.

I didn't particularly want to be subbed, but it was probably a good thing because I missed the mêlée at the end. It was a shame that all the reports about the trouble at the end of the match over-shadowed the fact that we had made it through to the final of the CIS Cup. After all the hard work, it was fantastic to know that we would be walking out at Hampden Park, but a more pressing matter was facing Rangers again in four days' time.

Claudio Reyna and Michael Mols and our own Lubo Moravcik had all been sent off for violent conduct and were suspended. Mr O'Neill was telling the players to stay cool and there was lots of talk in the papers about feuds between players and tensions rising. For me personally there was absolutely no feeling that there was a problem between the two sets of players. We played a hard game and that was it. It was time to prepare for the next one.

There was also a lot of talk about this match being the championship decider. There is no doubt it was very important, but with around 10 league games still left to play, a lot of things could change. It's only at the end of the season when you look back that you can really see the games that were crucial. Perhaps this was one of them. All I could think about at the time was that it was another game that needed to be won.

That said, all the talk of the championship before the match helped to give Celtic Park a real party atmosphere. We came out to the sound of singing and we started fairly brightly to keep things upbeat. Rangers began in positive mood with three up front, because they knew it was a bit of a do-or-die mission. Losing this match would leave them seriously adrift.

I tried an overhead kick that flew a long way over the bar, but five minutes later I flicked on a pass from Chris Sutton to Alan Thompson, who scored. I read later that that was our 100th goal of the season, but it certainly didn't register at the time. It was the goal that put us ahead against Rangers and that was all that mattered.

At half-time, we spoke about keeping our heads and remembering that the best form of defence is attack. If there was one thing we'd learnt from the previous game, it was that there was little point trying to sit back and defend that lead.

Suddenly, in the second half, a thunderstorm broke out – rain lashed down and somehow the electricity in the air seemed to charge us up. We picked up the pace and took the game to Rangers again. As the surface became more and more slippery, both sides started trying their luck from long range, but the keepers kept their concentration and stood firm and we were happy with a 1–0 win and three more points to tuck away.

Driving home with music playing in the car, I felt all the pressure of the previous week melting away. We hadn't had a chance to think about anything other than Rangers, and even the light training sessions we had done between the cup and SPL games had had an

I may not look happy, but I was. We'd just been presented with the SPL Championship trophy before beating Hearts 1–0.

Left: The 'no excuses' t-shirts were just a bit of a laugh.

Below: Some of the boys were slightly out of position here!

Bottom: The team spirit has been amazing this season – as you can see from our 'huddle' after beating St Mirren 1–0 and clinching the title.

Opposite top: It had been a long trek, and winning the title was a massive relief.

Opposite below: When I think of Celtic it's the fans I think of – they are the most amazing in the world.

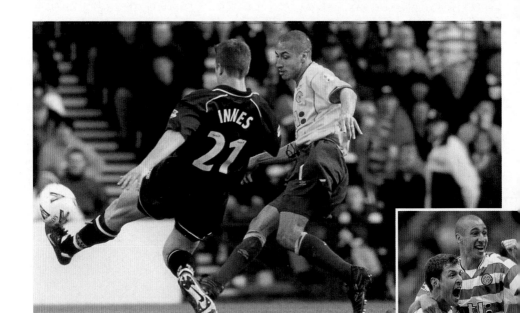

Above: To get a goal in a cup final is a dream come true, but to get your goal of the season (and this was mine) is really special.
Right: Like I said, Chris and I are close.
Below: Another great cross from Chris Sutton helped me score in the 3–1 Scottish Cup semi-final against Dundee United.

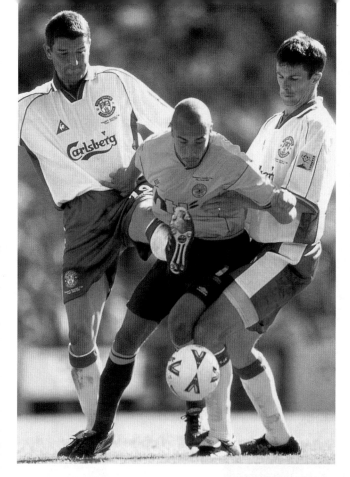

Above: Winning the Cup was the perfect end to a perfect season.
Left: I'm getting close attention from the Hibs' defence here in the cup.
Below: *Championes!* It's great to know that nobody can take it away from you.

BANK OF SCOTLAND
2000 - 2001   CHAMPIONS

Top: Martin O'Neill has to take a huge amount of credit for Celtic securing the treble.
Left: Playing for your country is always a great honour, with luck we'll be heading for the World Cup Finals. This 2–0 win over Slovakia helped.

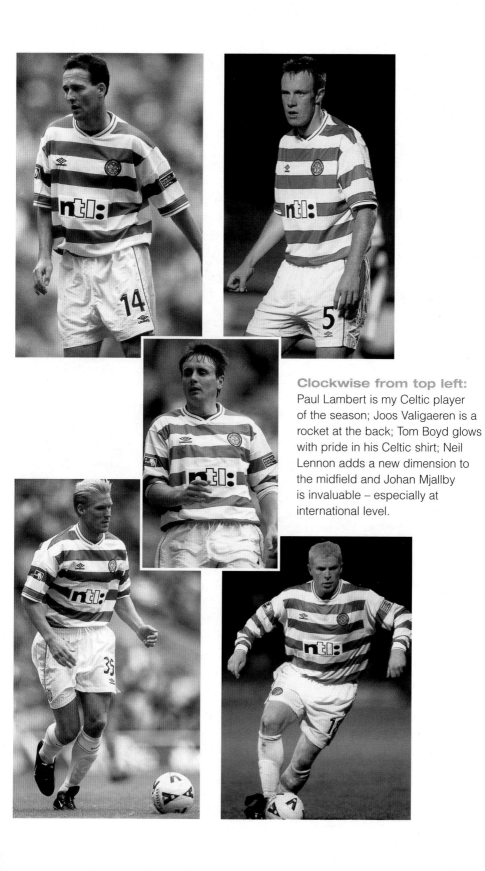

Clockwise from top left: Paul Lambert is my Celtic player of the season; Joos Valigaeren is a rocket at the back; Tom Boyd glows with pride in his Celtic shirt; Neil Lennon adds a new dimension to the midfield and Johan Mjallby is invaluable – especially at international level.

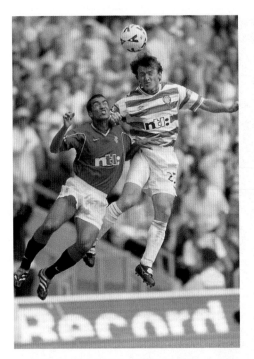

Top left: Lubo is a great competitor
and a good friend.

Top right: Stubbsie is a real character,
he has fought and beaten a terrible illness.
I wish him luck at Everton.

Above: Bobby Petta is a player who has
really shown what he can do this season.

Right: Stilian Petrov had a brilliant season
until his injury, but he is fighting back and
will return stronger than ever.

edge to them. But the best thing was that we had succeeded in concentrating on each game, one at a time, and had come away with all the spoils.

Within a few days we were in action again – and it was another big game. We travelled to Dunfermline for a Scottish Cup fourth round tie, and met a side that refused to give up. It was 1–1 with three minutes to go when Chris played a beautiful ball back to me which I chipped over the keeper. We thought that was it, but they equalized with virtually the last kick of the game.

It was 17 February and the replay was set for the 7 March, but three days earlier we played them in the league and were able to gain a psychological advantage by beating them 3–0. It told in the replay with a 4–1 win, including two for me from the spot. However, the games were piling up and the workload was beginning to take its toll. Players were starting to pick up injuries that they were not getting a chance to recover from. In the 1–0 win over Motherwell at Celtic Park on 21 February, Bobby Petta suffered quite a bad groin injury. It was a blow for him, because he had just been named in a 25-man squad for the Dutch national team.

In our next home match, we finally surrendered our 100 per cent home record when we drew 1–1 with Hibs. Johan Mjallby gave us the lead in the 22nd minute, and we really should have wrapped the game up, but Mark Libbra scored the equalizer with five minutes to go. Of course, it was a disappointment. We realized the significance of the result and, although I suppose it had to happen some time, we knew we were very good at home and we were proud of that record. It didn't feel right to drop points. We should have had it tied up, but they had two chances and scored on one of them.

Four days after knocking Dunfermline out of the Scottish Cup, we played the quarter-final against Hearts and won 1-0. We weren't at our best, although we had loads of possession. Sometimes you can almost have too much of the ball and for some reason lack ideas about what to do with it. I got on the end of Alan Thompson's cross to score in the 40th minute and in the end we were quite happy to walk off the pitch having ground out a win.

Every game seemed crucial now. The CIS Cup final was exactly one week later, but before we could think about walking out at Hampden against Kilmarnock, we had to play St Johnstone away, a game that had been postponed from earlier in the year because of freezing fog. It was hardly ideal preparation for a cup final, but we did the job expected of us by winning 2–1 and, with Rangers going down 2–0 at home to Dundee, our lead at the top stretched to 16 points.

But the game will be remembered by everyone who was there for the terrible injury to Stilian Petrov. Stan, as we call him, suffered a broken leg very similar to mine. It was a clean break of the tibia and fibula. I saw him charging forward and then a tackle went in and the next moment he was lying on his back with his leg in the air, holding his foot. At the moment the tackle went in, I heard a loud bang. It was so similar to what had happened to me that the memories came flooding back.

I ran over to see what he'd done, hoping that it wasn't as bad as my head was telling me. The way he was holding his leg I thought he had injured his ankle, then the medics appeared and it became obvious that it was pretty bad. Stan was stretchered off, and, as soon as the final whistle went, we just gave a quick wave to the fans, and sprinted into the dressing rooms to see how Stan was doing. The fact that he was still there was a bad sign. We were told the leg was broken, and Stan was rushed to Perth's Royal Infirmary, before being transferred to Glasgow Hospital's orthopaedic unit.

I knew he would be in the hands of the same people who had looked after me, and that gave me a lot of confidence. I was sure he would come back stronger than before. I had learned that, when you are injured like that, you just have to be a realist and there is no point dwelling on how or why the injury happened. You have to focus on getting fit again. The sooner you accept what has happened, the sooner you can start getting back.

Everybody in the team was sad for Stan and it did take away some of the excitement of going to the final a few days later . I think to some extent we sort of dedicated the final to Stan, and to the other players like Morten and Stubbsie, who were out for a long time. You don't exactly think, 'I'm going to win the cup for such-and-such,' because you are always thinking of the club first. You go out to win for Celtic and after that you do it for yourself, but you do also think of those unfortunate players who you know deserve all the medals and awards as much as you.

I had to laugh when I heard people suggest that we were doing so well in the league and cups simply because Rangers were suffering with injuries. What with Paul, Joos, Morten, Stubbsie, Bobby and Stilian, you couldn't exactly say we'd got off lightly in that respect. And now Chris was doubtful for the final against Kilmarnock. He'd hurt his shoulder in the league match at Dunfermline and I was hoping he would make a recovery in time to give us the option of a big physical presence up front. Otherwise, we faced going into that cup final without a major asset.

chapter ten
cup winners

The fact that we were playing so many games meant that there wasn't the sort of build-up to the CIS Cup final as you would normally get for a game of that importance. We really weren't able to think about the match until we had walked off the pitch against St Johnstone the Wednesday before.

Although every player obviously wanted to be involved in the cup final, there was never any question of us saving ourselves, holding back, in those games leading up to the big day at Hampden. You just can't think like that, and anyway it is a high risk policy. If you allow yourself to coast in this league you will lose, and winning is a habit that you have to keep up so that it's there for the big games. One question that you get asked a lot before any big game is, 'Are you confident?' I find the question hard to answer, because I don't know exactly what it means. If I were asked whether I had confidence in my teammates, I would definitely answer yes, of course. And I'd give the same answer if I was asked whether I had confidence in my own ability. I'd say yes, again ,if asked whether the team was going to try to play to the best of its ability. But there is no way you can make a prediction as to whether you will win or not.

You can say you desperately want to win, or you believe you have the talent in your team to win, but how can you predict the future? I've played too many games where luck, refereeing decisions, or a moment of inspiration has dictated the result. Some people perhaps think I'm too laid back in my attitude if I'm not saying, 'Yeah, of course we'll win'. Well, I never feel less than 100 per cent committed, but I'm a footballer, not a psychic.

After the St Johnstone game, we were in at the training ground at Barrowfield for a warm down the next day and then a couple of very light training sessions over the following days. I pretty much followed my usual routine, getting up shortly before I needed to go out and having a glass of juice or a bowl of porridge if I had time. I'd drive to the Park where I'd meet the other players and hang around chatting over a cup of coffee for a while before we'd all drive the short distance to training.

Despite all those games, I was feeling good, fit and sharp. Perhaps there is some law that says that if you have suffered a serious injury, you get a break afterwards and don't pick anything up for a while. Of course, there are always little knocks and minor strains and pulls. It is impossible to play professional football every week and not be constantly carrying minor stuff. But you get used to that.

On the day before the match I rested in the morning before saying goodbye to my family and driving to the hotel. By now my mind was totally focused on the final. The year before, while I was injured, I had had to sit on the bench while the boys went out and won the CIS Cup in front of the massed ranks of Celtic fans at Hampden. Obviously I was really happy for them, and they were great at making me feel a part of things, but I wanted to play. Now it felt great that I was going to be given an opportunity to play in a cup final just a year later. It would have been awful if I'd missed my only chance.

Although I tried not to start the season with any dreams of what we might achieve, in the back of my mind was the desire to win something, to make all those months of fighting back to fitness mean something tangible. It might be true that the CIS Cup is the lesser of the three domestic trophies, but that doesn't mean that it isn't something you badly want to win. Celtic were the holders and the cup looked pretty good in the trophy room, in a glass case, spotlit and quite beautiful. When you have it, it feels like it belongs to you and you don't want anyone else to get their hands on it. When you don't have it, you want it.

The papers were full of talk of this being the first of a possible treble of trophies for us, and the fact that it would be the first piece of silverware for Mr O'Neill at Celtic. We knew it would be great to get something in the trophy room again, but we never thought for one moment, 'We need to win this just in case it's the only thing we do win.' We wanted to win the cup because it was the next thing in our path. We wanted to win it because it would mean a great deal to the club and to the fans, and because it's a long way to the final only to lose when you get there.

We had our walk and then I got stuck into my usual pre-match spaghetti bolognese. As we travelled to Hampden Park through the streets of Glasgow, we started to pass supporters on their way to the ground. There seemed to be a huge number of Celtic fans on the move and I watched them, thinking how we shared a sense of excitement and nervous expectation. Seeing their faces, especially the young kids, fired me with the determination to do well, to put on a show and to play out of my skin.

Hampden's a superb ground and, filled with Celtic supporters on a cup final day, it can become a real cauldron of noise. But the changing rooms are sound-proof, so it isn't until you are in the tunnel on the way out that you are hit by the full impact of the crowd.

We arrived at the stadium in our grey club suits and after a short while wandered out to have a look at the pitch and soak up the atmosphere. The first bands of supporters were arriving, hours before kick-off, to make the most of the occasion. Then slowly the seats started to fill and the flags and shirts began to give the stands the look of a huge, green and white collage. I could have stood for ages watching the changing face of the stadium, but we were called back into the changing room to make all the final preparations for the game.

There was a lot of chat in the changing room, it's not a solemn place, and there was the smell of Deep Heat and the noise of studs scraping on the floor. I pulled at my boots to make sure they were nice and supple before I put them on and then laced them pretty tight. Some players have all sorts of rituals with their boots, but not me. All that matters is that they are comfortable. I normally go through a couple of pairs of boots a season, which I'm given by my sponsors, Umbro, and I just break them in during training.

Suddenly the room fell silent as the manager called for our attention and started running through what was expected of us. We didn't talk a great deal about the opposition, the feeling was that the most important thing we should know was exactly what we were going to do. Roles and formations were run over and everybody was left with a clear idea of their task. Although I was acutely aware of the importance of the occasion, and what it would mean to everyone if we won, I tried not to let my thoughts drift to the end of the match. I didn't want to be daydreaming during the game about lifting the cup just as a cross came over, so I forced myself to concentrate.

Since being called back into the changing room, everything had happened really quickly and it seemed like no time before we were being led out by Mr O'Neill. You could see how proud and excited he was; it was a fantastic reflection on him and his coaching team. The combination of new training methods, clearer goals and strong leadership was paying off and had bred a happy atmosphere within the camp. And a happy atmosphere tends to bring success.

As we walked out of the tunnel we were greeted by the sound of around 35,000 Celtic fans cheering, and what hair I had left on the back of my neck began to prickle. Those last few minutes before the game kicks off are always the worst for me. That is when I just want things to get going and I barely notice the formalities.

Chris Sutton and Bobby Petta had passed late fitness tests and we also had young Colin Healy in the starting line-up. Paul Lambert was showing no signs of his injury and, as I looked around the pitch, I saw myself surrounded by friends. Just for a second it reminded me of those matches down the bottom of my garden when I was a kid.

My father reckons I was kicking a ball from the moment I first made it onto two feet. I was 16 months old when I was given my first football and, as I grew up, games dominated our play time.

I loved swimming and in the winter I'd skate on the frozen ponds and play ice hockey, but it was football that was my real love and the games that I'd play in the middle of about 50 other young kids in the grassy field behind my garden would be the happiest memories of my childhood.

There has always been a lot of English football on Swedish TV, especially Liverpool and Spurs, and on Sunday afternoons I'd watch the likes of Kenny Dalglish, Graham Souness, Terry McDermott and Ossie Ardiles, and I would dream of being just like them, of scoring goals in cup finals. As soon as the programme finished, we'd all be outside recreating the great moves from the games. My parents bought me a video of Pele and I watched it again and again. When teachers asked the kids what they wanted to do when they grew up, most said things like a train driver or a fireman, but I always said a footballer. They would just laugh at me. I suppose it is the sort of thing kids say, but so few ever get to achieve.

The ref blew to start the game and a high ball was lofted over the midfield. The calls of the players were drowned out by the singing coming down from the stands. Nobody wanted to make an early mistake, so it was all a bit cautious and edgy, both sides sounding each other out and trying not to give anything away. The early nerves were taking their toll, with passes going astray and people flying into tackles to try to get the adrenaline flowing.

After only 10 minutes Bobby Petta pulled up, obviously in a lot of pain. He'd been on the receiving end of some stiff challenges and he had to be replaced by young Stephen Crainey. The fans gave Bobby a great round of applause as he left the field and my heart went out to him, being denied yet another important match. But

there wasn't time to dwell on sentiment and soon I found myself
running up and down the pitch looking for the ball. I needed to get
into the game. Sometimes, if the opposition defence is pushing up
and squeezing the midfield, the best thing a striker can do is drop
deeper to draw the defence out, leaving gaps in behind them.

Kilmarnock were working hard to deny us any rhythm and they
succeeded in keeping us quiet in front of goal in the first half. Our
first real effort was a free-kick from Lubo Moravcik after 15
minutes, and he had another shot saved by Gordon Marshall 10
minutes later. I thought I was in on goal when I managed to get
clear of their defence, but I was called offside by the linesman, and
a great free-kick from Stephen Crainey had my heart leaping for a
second as it rippled the side netting. But after what felt like a matter
of minutes, the half-time whistle blew.

We weren't too disappointed going in at half-time with the score
still at 0-0. We had created more chances than Kilmarnock and had
established a solid platform at the back. They had been putting everything into stopping us and we knew that they couldn't keep up that
sort of physical effort for long. I walked back to the tunnel feeling
sure that they would start to make mistakes in the second half.

As I jogged back out for the second half, I had no idea it was
going to start in the most perfect way. Practically from the kick-off,
Stephen Crainey and Neil Lennon combined to put the ball through
to Chris Sutton, who played a brilliant pass to Colin Healy. You just
have a feeling sometimes that a move is really on and you can hear
the expectation rise in the crowd. Colin drifted in from the right
and drove a low, hard shot against the legs of Marshall. The ball
spun out for a corner, but our tails were up and you could tell there

was a touch of nervousness in the Killies' defence. Lubo swung over a great cross which big Ramon Vega won in the air. As the ball fell, I swung a boot at it to catch it on the volley. My connection felt totally sweet and the ball flew into the net.

I had already started my celebration before the ball hit the net, and after a few seconds the cheers of the crowd were muffled by my teammates jumping on top of me. Moments like that are priceless. You want to pinch yourself just to make sure it is all true. Even after all these years of playing as a professional footballer, one of my first thoughts when something like that happens is a sense of relief that I'm doing my job, proving that I am good enough to be in this team, on this pitch. It's really important to any professional to believe that his teammates respect him.

Although the goal settled us, it also made us back off a little bit. Whether you mean to or not, the desire to protect your lead seems to make you sit back instinctively. And it all seemed to be going wrong 10 minutes later when we lost Chris Sutton to a red card. It's hard to say whether it was deserved or not, certainly it was a clumsy challenge, but I think Chris was just a bit slow going into the tackle. I think referees should think very carefully before sending somebody off in a cup final. It is such an important game and it's only fair to the fans to see an even contest. I suppose with so much attention on such a game, the referee is keen not to let anything go unpunished.

It was a boost to Kilmarnock. I knew that I would have to go looking for the ball more and that there wasn't as much chance that I would be getting the kind of constant service that makes my job a lot easier. But it certainly didn't stop us going in search of more goals if the opportunity came our way.

With 10 men you know that you have to keep things tight and there is no way that you can just start throwing people into attack. There was a little bit of reorganisation and we knew we would have to keep our passing game going, try to keep the ball away from Kilmarnock and make them work. There was still half an hour left, more than enough time for them to take advantage of their extra man. What we needed badly was a lucky break – and that is just what we got.

Lubo found a bit of space and then played a brilliant ball through to me. As I shot it, the ball took a bad deflection off one of the Killie defenders and looped over the keeper. It may not have been the most beautiful of goals, but in the record books it will count just as much as if it had been a 30-yard free-kick, curled around the defensive wall.

It was exactly what we needed at that moment, a touch of luck that gave us some breathing space and meant Kilmarnock would have to start throwing everything forward. There was now about 15 minutes left and they would have to abandon all caution if they were going to get anything out of the game.

To be honest, I think that goal really took the wind out of them. To concede a goal when you are a man up is quite a blow, and I could see a few heads starting to drop. Our fans were now in full voice, urging us on for one final push. There was a chorus of, 'There's only one Stan Petrov', in tribute to our injured teammate. Fans have this fantastic sense of occasion that can be very moving at times.

A few minutes later, there was a bit of a scramble in midfield and when the ball found its way over to me, I brought it down and looked around to see what was on. For some reason, it appeared like everybody else had stopped, so I decided to push it forward and see what would open up. The defence was a little bit square and I was able to get beyond it with the first surge. The cover came over, but as the defender challenged for the ball I held him off and kept running towards goal.

By the time I reached the penalty area, I was pretty tired and I could feel my legs getting heavy. I had left my teammates behind, so there was absolutely no chance that I could release the ball to anybody else. I needed to do something because my legs were about to give out. I faked to play it into the far corner, but I couldn't really hit it there because the defender was coming across and the keeper had it covered. So instead I dragged it around the keeper with the sole of my boot and rolled the ball gratefully into the net.

If I hadn't been so tired I think I might have hurried everything and possibly lost the chance. As it was, my mind was working quickly, but everything I was doing was with great deliberation. There is no way I had thought about scoring a goal like that when I had picked the ball up in my own half. In fact, I had no idea what I was going to do at all. All I knew was that, by pushing forward, I would be able to open things up and something might develop. By the time I reached the penalty area, I had decided I was going to have a shot and then I reacted to what was happening around me.

Okay, I know that I'm always saying it doesn't matter who scores, so long as Celtic win, and if I score I don't mind whether it is a 30-yard chip or it bounces off the back of my heel. That's true almost all the time, but to get a goal like that in the cup final is an absolutely amazing feeling. It really is the stuff that dreams are made of, the kind of goal you score when you're a kid playing with your mates and imagining you are doing it in a cup final. Having said that, I don't think it would have felt so good if we had then gone on to lose 4–3!

As I ran back to my teammates I was so tired that my celebration was only a fraction of what I felt inside. We knew that there really was no way back for Kilmarnock now. We weren't about to sacrifice a three-goal lead. I looked over at the bench and saw that there were only about five minutes to go. The players and staff were all straining, waiting for the final whistle so that they could run on to the pitch and start the celebrations.

Kilmarnock were still playing football, in that way you do when you know you're unlikely to win, but want to get something out of the game. Equally we were determined not to give a goal away and just wanted to keep possession as much as possible. Every short blast of the whistle we hoped would be the end of the match, and when the whistle did finally go we threw our arms in the air and grabbed each other. The manager came on and patted us all on the back, shaking us by the hand.

I always want to stop at moments like that, to just pause and drink in everything that is going on around me, so that I can remember every single second of it. Sometimes you see players walk away from the rest of the team, just so they can have a moment to themselves to remember. Of course, what happens most of the time is that you forget to stop and think and just get carried away in the celebrations, and have to look at the video afterwards to remember exactly what it was you did – and hope it wasn't too embarrassing.

One of the happiest looking players was Chris Sutton. Obviously he was disappointed at being sent off, but I think he was very happy that it hadn't cost us. I know that he would have been kicking himself for a very long time if we had lost because he wasn't on the pitch. He had that 'Cheers, mate' look on his face.

We were all cheering and we went over to the fans who were cheering back at us. We started to do a lap of honour and I could feel a little cramp in my legs as we jogged around the pitch. But it was nothing too bad and certainly wasn't going to stop me paying tribute to our fantastic fans. It was their triumph too and we wanted to show them how much we appreciated everything they had done and all the support they had given us.

It's a great feeling lifting the trophy. It's another one of those things you practise as a kid – holding the cup aloft, kissing it, showing it to the fans. It's bizarre when you find yourself actually doing it for real and you hear the roar of the crowd as you hold the cup by its ears.

Back in the changing room there was a great atmosphere, champagne was flowing and everyone was hugging each other. We were all trying to speak at the same time. As I sat taking my boots off, John Robertson, who is a great joker, came over to me and said, 'Henrik, when are you going to stop panicking so much in front of goal?' Everybody cracked up.

Eventually we headed back to Celtic Park with the cup and met up with all our families, the rest of the staff, club directors and other guests. It was a bit of time to enjoy our achievement amongst ourselves and reflect on what we had done, in our ancestral home. The Cup was put back in its rightful place and I know the following day Mr O'Neill took it to show Stan, who had been told that he was likely to need an operation, rather than just having the leg set, and could be out of the game for up to 10 months. Despite his disappointment at not being able to play a part in the game, Stan was really pleased for us and he knew that he was instrumental in that win.

We headed off from the Park to a restaurant, with more champagne and great food but, unfortunately, I had to leave at about midnight as my teammates partied on, because I had a 6.45am flight the following morning to hook up with the Swedish international squad for a friendly against Malta. And I'd completely forgotten to pack.

chapter eleven
the treble

Now the only domestic trophy that I had not managed to get my hands on since arriving in Scotland was the Scottish Cup. I suppose it's pretty natural to desperately want something you don't have and, in a season like the one we were having, greed for silverware can start to take hold of you.

We'd had a pretty tough route to the final. We'd been taken to a replay by a determined Dunfermline side back in February and had had a narrow 1–0 win over Hearts in the fifth round. The semi-final had been a real battle against Dundee United, one of the teams we'd been having trouble with all season, but, as soon as the final whistle had gone and we'd won 3–1, it was great to know we'd booked another trip back to Hampden Park.

It was an amazing spell. Only four weeks had passed since our CIS Insurance Cup triumph and in between we had clinched the league title with a 1–0 win at home to St Mirren. That was the sort of season we were having. Important games seemed to be falling over each other. We never really seemed to get the chance to take a breath, and think about what we were doing. Every victory was followed by another important match.

I hadn't scored since my hat-trick in the CIS Cup Final, but we had shown our depth of goalscoring talent in beating Aberdeen away and then Dundee and St Mirren at home, all by the odd goal. Tommy Johnson had got vital goals in the last two matches and, with five league games left to play, we had achieved our first aim of beating Rangers to the championship.

Even after winning the league title, we only allowed ourselves a brief celebration before it was back down to business. Mr O'Neill made it clear that we still had a very important match ahead with the semi-final. There was never any feeling that we had done enough. True we had won two trophies and that would satisfy us, but we still wanted the Scottish Cup badly and it was the next target ahead of us.

We were aware that we were on for an historic treble – the papers wouldn't let us forget it – and we thought we had a good chance of winning the cup. By that stage of the season we had no doubts about our ability, or about the sort of commitment we were capable of, but we certainly weren't going to get carried away. Some newspapers and other commentators seemed to think it would be a formality, that we would simply have to turn up and win the cup. We laughed it off.

Having got past Dundee United, we were to face Hibernian, a side that had proved its calibre by sticking with the title race and would end up finishing third, an impressive achievement for a pretty small squad. They were packed with quality players, like their captain, Franck Sauzee, also Marc Libbra,and Mixu Paatelainen. Quality ran through their whole side, there was no area of weakness.

I think there are some similarities between ourselves andHibs – in the way we both play as a tight unit, as a close-knit team where everyone works hard for one another. It is great to be in a side where you know that players are unselfish and will play to your strengths. I know, for instance, that if I can get into good positions to score, the ball will come to me. And my teammates know what I'm doing and where I am heading when I set off on a run. You don't often find yourself in space and the ball nowhere near, or without support.

Hibs had twice held us to a draw during the season and no one had taken more points off us. They were good going forward, always full of ideas and, like us, they were very strong at the back; you knew that you were going to have to work for every opening.

The fact we beat Hibs 5–2 on 6 May, less than three weeks before the final, meant absolutely nothing in respect of what would happen at Hampden. I suppose there may have been some sort of psychological effect on the Hibs players, I don't know, but I'm sure we all knew that the cup final would be something totally different. We knew that after a really good season they were facing the prospect of finishing up empty handed, and they would be desperate to have something to show for all their hard work.

Since clinching the championship, we had beaten Hearts and Rangers, against whom I'd scored my 50th goal of the season, but the Hibs game was our last league win. I took my league tally to 35, but I was hoping there were more saved away for the final. The following week, we lost 2–0 at home to Dundee and then, six days before the final, we went to Kilmarnock and lost 1–0. As usual, we had trained on Friday morning, but before that the whole club had gone to St Columbkille's Church in Rutherglen for Bobby Murdoch's funeral.

It was a shock to everybody at the club when Bobby died. He was regarded with enormous affection and respect for his part in the Lisbon Lions' side that won the European Cup in 1967 and there were a number of people around the Park, like John Clark, his ex-teammate, who had been good friends of Bobby. The Lisbon Lions are a massive part of Celtic history and you don't have to be at the club for very long before you feel a part of that heritage. There are other players from that team, like the Wee Man Jimmy Johnstone, who I've met and become friends with. They are a very special group of guys, wonderful characters and great footballers. Bobby had been such an important member of that side and will always be a legend at Celtic Park.

It was sad to see so many of the great older players upset, having lost one of their closest friends, and it made me feel quite humble. It took a strong will to get back on the training pitch and start preparing for the game against Kilmarnock.

We did a bit of running and played a couple of practice knock-arounds, nothing too strenuous. There were just a few minutes left and most of us were starting to think about getting away, when I stretched for a ball and felt a small pull in my hamstring. I immediately pulled up and called over to say that I thought I had better stop. It didn't feel particularly bad, but a hamstring is the sort of injury that is easy to aggravate if you are not really careful. The last thing I was going to do was risk my place in the cup final.

I received some treatment straight away, and later that afternoon I could feel a dull ache in the muscle. Still, I wasn't worried and felt confident that, as long as I treated the leg properly, I would make a quick recovery.

I was one of five regular first team players who were not in the side against Kilmarnock. We took a bit of stick for the defeat ,but it's wrong to say that we weren't taking the match seriously. That isn't the Celtic way. Of course, our priority at that stage was the cup final, but we certainly wanted to win every game and we always believe you should show your opponents respect. If I had been fully fit, I would have been up for selection, but it was obvious that the only thing I could do was rest. Anyone who had any sort of injury wasn't going to be risked in our last game before the cup final.

But losing our last two league games of the season was still a disappointment. Until the last few weeks of the season we'd only lost the one game, against Rangers, and until the Dundee game we were unbeaten at home in the league. We would have liked to have finished our campaign on a high, but Kilmarnock were up for it and they deserved to beat us.

There were worries over injuries to Bobby, Chris and Lubo, although I had a funny feeling that they would all pull through. We certainly wanted to be able to go into the game with our strongest possible selection. I spent the whole weekend resting my leg, keeping mobile so there would be no stiffening, but not putting any strain on it at all. On Tuesday I went in to training and just did a bit of jogging.

Even though I wasn't really worried, there is always that little part at the back of your mind that fears something might be wrong. So it was great when I was able to jog and felt no problem at all with the hamstring. I didn't feel anything and, when I put a bit more into it the following day, I knew that I was fine and available for selection for the cup final squad – and made sure Mr O'Neill knew straight away.

It was only then that I let my mind stretch as far as Saturday's final. Knowing that I would be able to play was a huge weight off my shoulders. By Thursday I was back training with the group and totally involved in all the preparation and build up. Everybody was very aware that this was the end of the road that had started way back in August, and we could sense the moment, we were anxious for the day to arrive. The treble was there, just one game away, and to miss out on it now would take the gloss off a very good season.

In the days leading up to the game, you start concentrating more and more on what you are going to face. It's quite difficult getting through those times, because all you really want is for the game to start. All the everyday things in life seem unimportant. There is nothing you can do until you are on the pitch, and the time seems to drag until the kick off.

Eventually Friday arrived, and we all met up at the Park; then headed off to the hotel where we would spend the night before the game. I was feeling very relaxed and it was a feeling that had spread through the whole squad. There were jokes flying about and everyone was having a laugh.

The day before a cup final is a time for togetherness, a time to feel part of one big, happy family, all striving for the same goal and all going through the same feelings. We were becoming quite used to the experience of being on the verge of triumph, but the thrill of it hadn't worn off.

That night in the hotel everybody was resting and trying to relax. A few guys were sitting around talking about the game, others were reading the papers. I was playing PlayStation, just to try to distract myself. Although I say I was relaxed, I also just wanted to get on with the game. I would have played Hibs that night if I could.

The manager was leaving it right to the last moment to make sure that the injured players were okay, and in the end Bobby Petta was the only one who didn't make it. That was the story of his season: a key player who was denied the big occasions. I really felt for him.

The hours before kick-off are when the nerves get you. We'd been through the usual match-day routine – the walk, the spaghetti bolognese – and now it was just a case of waiting. People were saying we might be overconfident. What do they think you are going to do on the pitch if you are 'overconfident?' It's not like you ever take it easy because you expect to win, you always have to go out and make the win happen. We knew we would have to work hard, as we had all season. There would be no let-up now.

Once we were on the way to Hampden Park, I was feeling much better. It was a beautiful day, the sun was shining and I had to squint to see the supporters making their way to the ground. This is what being a professional footballer is all about, being part of a huge, noisy family and knowing you have the opportunity to make that family proud.

We walked out in our suits to look at the pitch, which was in a better condition than it had been for a while. We watched the ground filling up and then headed back to the changing rooms. In what seemed like no time at all, we were back on the pitch.

At last the moment had just about arrived, but even those few minutes before kick-off can feel like a lifetime. You warm up and stand for the formalities, thinking, 'Come on, I just want to play now.' And finally the moment arrived.

Hibs certainly hadn't been reading any of the papers that said Celtic only had to turn up to get the cup, or if they had read the papers, they had been motivated by them. We had a close call when Libbra set up John O'Neil whose shot only narrowly missed our left-hand post. After about a quarter of an hour, Lubo was injured in a challenge and signalled to the bench that he needed to come off. He had a badly gashed knee and there was no way that he could carry on. It looked like he had re-opened an old wound. It meant that we had lost a key player, but in his place came Jackie McNamara, who was to prove a vital ingredient.

Both sides were playing good football. There was a tough battle going on in midfield, but front players were being released and chances were being created. With about 30 minutes gone, I managed to get on to a stray pass by Hibs for a shot on goal, but I put it in the side netting. Then, a few minutes later, Jackie scored. Didier Agathe did well out on the right before slipping the ball through to Jackie who ran on into the penalty area and shot home.

As soon as the ball hit the net, a roar went up from the crowd and we rushed to congratulate Jackie. It was the breakthrough that we felt we needed. You never expect to score early in a cup final because both sides normally start quite cautiously, but as the first half wears on you really want to get a goal to make sure that the opposition have to do the chasing. We had another chance just before half-time when Didier teased a way through the Hibs defence and released the ball to me, but unfortunately I couldn't quite collect it.

We went in at half-time reasonably happy. I was really thirsty and just welcomed the chance to get a drink. The gaffer was telling us to keep our heads, to keep playing football and not let them back into the game. The break had come at a bad time for us because we were on top, but we knew it was important to start the second half the way we had finished the first. And we were determined not to sit back.

Luckily, we didn't have long to wait before putting ourselves further ahead. Jackie and Chris linked up on the left and, when I saw what they were doing, I started to make my run into the box. I pulled towards the back post, but suddenly realized Jackie was shaping to cross the ball short and on the ground. I paused for a second, until I saw him get into exactly the right position,. Then, as he drew his leg back, I darted forward, while a defender behind me seemed to slip and I was there to meet the ball with my left foot. The ball shot up into the top left corner of the net. It was one of those occasions when everything goes right. The shot had power behind it and I was able to direct it exactly where I wanted it to go. There was just a moment when I watched to see if the keeper could get to it, and then turned away, knowing it was there.

I felt a split second of personal joy and relief before hearing the ground erupt in a barrage of noise. I ran towards the Celtic support and saw a blur of faces and arms waving, scarves and flags. Within seconds the rest of the team were there and we were hugging and shouting at each other.

As we walked back to the centre circle, I did feel that perhaps we had done enough. I knew it would be really difficult for Hibs to come back from that. If we could keep playing football and not make any stupid mistakes, I'd soon be getting my hands on that trophy. It's a strange feeling when you sense glory during a game and you have to stop yourself getting carried away and losing concentration.

But now there was a little bit of breathing space, and as Hibs were forced to throw everything at us, they left a few gaps at the back that we could move into. I had a shot tipped away and then, with about 10 minutes to go, Chris knocked the ball to me and I ran on into the box. I was holding the defender off and trying to shape up to shoot. He knew he couldn't let me get any closer and brought me down.

I knew at once it was a penalty and was probably picking myself up and thinking about putting the ball on the spot before the referee even blew. With 10 minutes to go and being 2–0 up, I was probably more confident than I'd ever felt taking a penalty. I slotted it away and knew the game was over. The crowd noise went up another notch and stayed like that for the rest of the match. It was incredible playing in an atmosphere like that. The fans shared my belief that we had won and were singing away. I felt a part of this whole Celtic family. There were waves of joy coming down from the stands.

Those last few minutes actually went quite quickly and when the final whistle blew we just grabbed each other. It was the end of a long, hard season and we had managed to bring all three domestic trophies back to Celtic Park. It seemed almost unreal. At the start of the season, we hadn't dreamed of anything like this, we had just wanted to do well, better than the previous season, and close the gap on Rangers. By the end of this season, we had done all those things and more. Hampden Park was the second best place to finish the season, and the whole stadium was rapidly becoming a huge Celtic party.

We have always played as a team, as a good unit. Everybody will tackle back and defend if they have to, and every player will push forward and support the attack if they need to. Our work rate has been incredible. That is partly down to the sort of training we have been doing and also the spirit and friendship among the players. When you have that bond, you don't think twice about working for each other and you don't give people stick if they make a mistake.

I went towards our defenders because I knew they had been so important in what we had achieved. Not only had they stopped attackers getting through all season, but they had created chances by supporting the midfield, and knowing you have that quality at the back allows the rest of the team to press up and be aggressive.

I was so happy at that moment and as I looked around my teammates and friends, I saw that they were just grinning stupidly at each other. We started running around to the Celtic fans, but I have to say that it isn't true that you don't feel tired when you win, I felt knackered and my legs were heavy. The difference is that you ignore the tiredness. We wanted to show the fans how much their support had meant to us and that all we had achieved was as much for them as it was for us.

I waited my turn to go up and hold the cup. I remember it glinting and looking beautiful with the green and white ribbons. I picked it up and showed it to the crowd as they roared again. Mr O'Neill was so pleased, he was slapping the players' backs and talking non-stop to everyone. It was great for him, he had worked so hard and had made such a difference to the team. Players who had not fulfilled their potential in the past were now among the best in the club.

We wanted to spend as long as we could sharing the experience with the fans, being out on the pitch and soaking up the fantastic atmosphere. Afterwards we were asked if it felt good to beat Rangers to everything. Well, yes, but it felt good to beat all the other teams in the SPL too. By the end we weren't really thinking about Rangers, just about what we had achieved.

Eventually, we had to go back into the changing room, where the laughing and joking carried on, and then we travelled back to the Park. All the back-room people were there, diehard Celtic fans who love the club and were so proud of what we had done. Everyone was happy and it was great to be surrounded by smiling people. After some years of having had to play the poor neighbour to Rangers, and not win anything, it was so good to know we deserve d what we had done.

Afterwards, we headed off to the same restaurant that we had gone to after the CIS Cup Final and had a great evening. You can't beat a bit of champagne, good food and having your friends and family around you when you have just won every possible honour in your league. It was a brilliant party, everybody from the club was there, and this time I was able to stay all night.

The following day, it all started to sink in. On Monday I was going to fly off to Sweden for some vital World Cup qualifiers, so Sunday was a time to relax, be with my family and enjoy looking back on a fantastic season. I spent most of the day playing with

Jordan, who has developed a good arm for throwing water-bombs, and we had a little lunch in the garden. That night I had to pack again, ready to fly to Sweden, but it was great knowing that I was going back to my homeland having achieved so much. Towards the end of my time at Feyenoord, I had worried about going home and being seen as a failure. There didn't seem much fear of that now.

chapter twelve
sweden

I was 22 when I got the call-up for my first Swedish cap. It was in November 1993, just two months after I had signed for Feyenoord. The game was against Finland in Stockholm, we won 3–2 and I scored. I remember it was a header from close range and the feeling was just unbelievable. I knew straight away that this was something I wanted to keep doing. There were a lot of good players around, players who I had looked up to, admired and wanted to learn from. Now I was running out with them. My family and friends were incredibly proud of me, especially my brothers Kim and Robert, who used to join in those huge kick-arounds as kids.

It was a very exciting time in my life. Everything seemed to be coming together with the career that I had feared for so long wasn't going to go anywhere at all. I was playing for one of the big European club sides and now I was playing for my country. The problems at Feyenoord were yet to come.

When I was a kid playing all-day matches with my brothers and friends in the fields near to where we lived, we all pretended to be great players. You would hardly ever score a goal or make a good pass without putting the name of one of your heroes on it. Some of my heroes were players from English clubs, like Kenny

Dalglish, Terry McDermott and Ossie Ardiles, but there were also great Swedish players who I would often pretend to be, scoring an important goal for my country. When you actually become a professional footballer your dreams get more ambitious. When you find yourself lifting the cups and league championship trophies and playing in big competitions for real, you become greedy for more.

The World Cup in the USA in 1994 made me eager to get to another World Cup tournament, and this time I wanted to be involved in every game. Having missed out on the 1998 World Cup in France, I desperately want us to make the 2002 World Cup in Japan and Korea, both for myself and because I wanted Sweden to be recognized as one of the top international sides. Remember we finished third in 1994. If you're going to play international football, you'll want to do it in the tournaments where the best teams and best players will be on show.

When the groups were drawn, we knew immediately that we had a tough task on our hands to qualify. There was a real mixed bag of quality and unknown quantities. I knew quite a lot about Turkey and Macedonia, but Moldova, Azerbaijan and Slovakia were all really strange to me.

In some ways you would prefer to play top sides that you know, rather than face the unknown. I thought there was a good chance that Turkey would be our main challenger for top spot. They have a lot of fine players, including Tugay, who I know well from our Old Firm encounters. Turkish club sides have made a real impact in Europe in recent years and you always know that they are going to be skilful and very passionate players. And the passion is echoed by the fans – you're guaranteed a noisy reception when you go there. They love their football and demand a lot from the team, which often means that the real pressure is on them.

There was a great deal of determination throughout our squad to qualify well, to do it in style and show the world what we were capable of. We had just come off the back of that very disappointing European Championship and it was a case of picking ourselves up and doing the job that we knew we could do. What I really wanted was to be able to go into a major international championship fully fit and as a first choice player. We knew we were a good side and we just wanted the opportunity to get out there and prove it, to the world in general and to the people back home in Sweden who doubted us. We knew we had to raise our game quite a few notches from Euro 2000, and we certainly didn't want to get into a cycle of defeats.

We had strength throughout the side and plenty of experience, with guys like Patrick Andersson, Anders Svensson, Fredrik Ljunberg, Roland Nilsson and even me. It is strange for me to think that I am one of the old hands of the squad now. I suppose I have become one of the players who are seen as veterans. It's great for me to have Johan Mjallby in the side because we know each other so well. We have a good understanding on the pitch and hopefully that helps our teammates as well.

At the start of September we had to travel to Baku in Azerbaijan. It was an amazing experience and, even though we were in and out of the country in two days, I still felt that I had done something very different. I would have struggled to find Azerbaijan on a map before we were drawn against them. I knew it had once been a part of the

Soviet Union and it was quite intriguing to find out what it's like there. The disadvantage was not knowing any of their players. I don't think any of them were playing for European clubs, so we had no idea what level they were at. We didn't know what sort of game they played and what facilities you could look forward to.

We first flew to Austria where we had a short training camp. It's important to bring all the players together and play a few practice games, so you can start getting used to each other again. It's always quite easy to slip back into playing with the Swedish team because they are quality footballers. If you have good players around you, it doesn't take long for everyone to work out how to play with each other, but what the coach has to do is mould a bunch of different talents into a cohesive team. That's a tough task because there's so little time for the coach to get a real sense of how he wants his team to play.

We looked at what videos there were of Azerbaijan and analysed their strengths and weaknesses. And then, before we knew it, we were on the plane to the former Soviet republic. We all had pre-conceived ideas of the place being poor and backward, so I was surprised to find that the hotel was one of the best I have ever stayed in. The facilities were fantastic and the staff were really helpful. It was evidence that the poor standard of living was not something shared by all. It's one of the great privileges of being a footballer that you get to go to these places and see for yourself what they are like. When Azerbaijan comes into the news in the future, shall have a better idea of what sort of culture is being talked about.

The ground was nothing special, but I can say for sure that I have played in much worse stadiums. Of course, you always want to play in ideal conditions, but you can't have Celtic Park every week. So this was like any average game abroad: the pitch was okay but nothing special, the crowd was quite noisy and we couldn't understand a word they were saying. You don't pay much attention to the details when you're out there playing, you just get on with your job. If you have a lot of support, you hear it, but if the only fans there are hostile, you just tune them out. I think there were about 15,000 people in the stadium, but because it was quite small it seemed a lot louder. The fact is, though, if you've played for Celtic against Rangers at Ibrox, it is unlikely that you are going to be intimidated by any crowd anywhere in the world.

We weren't outstanding, but we did enough to win 1–0 with a goal by Anders Svensson in the first 10 minutes, which allowed us to relax a little bit and not go chasing the game. It was a very physical game, but that was not a problem for any of us. The Swedish players are quite a big, strong bunch and my experience of football in Scotland means I know how to handle myself when the hard challenges come in.

Of course, you are always a little worried about picking up an injury in a match like that. It's bad enough getting injured playing for the club that pays your wages, but it's an unwelcome risk when you are on international duty. Celtic have always been brilliant about releasing me and I wouldn't want their generosity to backfire.

To travel to a place like Azerbaijan, against such an unknown quantity, and to come away with three points was pleasing, although there was room for improvement in our performance. We took a bit of stick from some of the press in Sweden, who expect us to go out and play like Brazil every time. I know footballers are always saying this these days, but it is naïve to think we can go out and win by three or four goals every time against so-called lesser opposition. When you play sides that aren't perhaps as technically strong, you still have to give them respect and be cautious. They all know how to defend, and if they just want to put up a barrier, you are in for an unspectacular game. The most important thing for us at that moment was to qualify for the World Cup. There would be little point in playing beautiful football and walking away empty handed. In the real world you ensure that you are going to win the game first.

Our next outing was to face Turkey in Gothenburg. We play our home games in both Gothenburg and Stockholm but, given the choice, I would always prefer to play in Stockholm. It's not that Gothenburg isn't a great stadium. In fact, the problem is that, in some ways, it is too good, and certainly too big. Even with a crowd of 40–45,000, which is normal for internationals against all but the top teams, Gothenburg is far from full. With the same size crowd in Stockholm, the ground is packed and there is a great atmosphere. I have always liked playing in front of big crowds that make a lot of noise and add a bit of atmosphere to the occasion, and I think that since I have been playing for Celtic, it has become even more important to me. You get so used to having that sort of support behind you that you start to think that all crowds should be like that. Swedish supporters are good. In many ways they are like British fans. They love football and really get behind the team, even when you're not doing brilliantly – unlike in some countries.

The match against Turkey was as tough as we expected it to be. Neither side was prepared to give anything away and it became a bit of a battle in midfield, with few chances being created. We went in at half-time 0–0 and the talk was all about trying to step it up a bit in the second half and press forward. After 69 minutes we managed to make the breakthrough and I was lucky enough to get the goal. The ball came over and I got my head to it, burying the ball in the corner. Some people had questioned my scoring record for Sweden, so it was nice to be able to show that I could do it at international level. I suppose, because I have scored so many at club level, people expect me to do the same for Sweden. Well, I think my record for Sweden is okay, but of course it is more difficult because the players around you don't know you as well. At Celtic, my teammates know when I'm likely to make a run and how I like to get the ball, and I know where to go when the ball is in a particular place. You can never develop that sort of understanding in the limited time you have with the international side.

What is more, I always believe that there is more to my game then scoring goals. I would like to think that I work hard and help out the rest of the team and support the other striker who I am playing with. It is unfair to judge any player on just one aspect of his game, even if that player is a striker and the main aspect of his role is his goals.

Unfortunately, on that night in Gothenburg, my goal wasn't enough. Well into injury time at the end of the game, Turkey got a penalty, and Tayfur Havutcu scored. It was a great disappointment. As soon as I saw their player go down, I waited to hear the whistle and felt my heart sink. We hadn't been brilliant again, but I thought we had played well enough to earn the victory. Against a well-organized Turkish side we had kept the game tight and taken one of the very few opportunities there had been. But we hadn't quite stuck it out to the very end.

We had the chance to pick ourselves up just a few days later with a trip to Slovakia and a game in the national stadium in Bratislava. Before these two games we had been looking to get a win at home and secure at least a point away. Now we needed something more, but Slovakia refused to be broken down. The game ended goalless and we were forced to listen to some of the critics who were already trying to write us off from the qualifying campaign. It was annoying because we'd played well in Bratislava and only a lack of ruthlessness had stopped us from getting the victory. Of course, you have to kill games off when you're on top and that is something that we all knew we'd need to work on. We were good in the first half, but sat back too much in the second.

I arrived home a wee bit tired and had to get some rest to be ready to take on St Mirren two days later. I would never for a moment think of not playing for my club after coming back from an international. Given the choice between playing football and not playing football, I'll always choose the game. The Swedish coach Tommy Soderberg was keen to get us together for some friendlies before our next World Cup qualifiers, to work on our ruthlessness and concentration. That meant that at the end of February, right after drawing 1–1 with Hibs at Celtic Park, I was on a flight to Sweden to hook up with the squad for a friendly in Malta.

Of course, the match itself wasn't that important, but it was a rare opportunity to try a few things out and work on some different combinations. I actually enjoyed the trip as a welcome break from the incredible pressure of the league, which had certainly begun to mount.

The ground in Valetta is quite small, nice enough, but hardly a cauldron of atmosphere. If any of the British teams play in Malta it gets packed, but they don't show a great deal of interest in most other sides. I think about 400 supporters turned up on the night, quite a contrast to running out in front of 60,000 at the Park. We disposed of Malta quite easily, 3–0, and it proved a worthwhile exercise. No matter who you play, a win is a win, and I think it did us good to get that winning feeling again.

Next up were two back-to-back qualifiers at the end of March, at home against Macedonia in Gothenburg and then away to Moldova. It meant I missed out on a break with some of the other Celtic guys, who were heading off to Spain and other sunny places for the week following the CIS Cup final, and I was just the tiniest bit jealous.

Macedonia made things difficult for us in Gothenburg, but we also made things difficult for ourselves. Anders Svensson scored just before half-time, for the only goal of the game, but this time we weren't satisfied with the win. We just didn't seem to click and we deserved the stick we got. But it was another three points, so we were still on course for qualification.

Moldova is a fascinating part of the world. I think it had just been named as the poorest country in Europe before we arrived, and you could see why. It can be a bit of a culture shock for someone like me who has lived in the relative affluence of Sweden, Holland and Scotland, to see how things are in a place like that. It really opens your eyes. It's hard to believe that you are still in Europe.

Again, though, the hotel belied the poverty of the country. It was lovely, with all the facilities we could have wished for. We had a light training session on the evening before the match and managed to iron out a few little problems. We played much better than we had against Macedonia and came away with a 2–0 win. Now I began to think how close qualification would be if we could just hold things together. We were beginning to look like the team we knew we could be and our confidence was very high.

The coach was anxious to take us to Switzerland at the end of April, to keep that momentum going, which was good thinking, but placed a heavy burden on me. Celtic had just clinched the SPL and there was still the Scottish Cup final to come. I'd been playing so many matches that I felt one more might just tip me over the edge. It's difficult weighing up the needs of club and country, and I'm just lucky that things have worked out okay. I don't think playing for Sweden has ever affected my Celtic performance negatively.

We beat Switzerland quite comfortably and then turned our attention to the serious business of preparing to play Slovakia in Stockholm, and Moldova in Gothenburg. First I had the Scottish Cup final, and then a day to bask in the glory of that victory before flying out to Sweden. I got a great reception from my international teammates for winning the treble and I was presented with a painting that had been signed by the whole team as a memento. It was very touching.

That was the first chance I had really had to let everything that had happened during the season sink in, and it felt wonderful. Now I planned to stay on in Sweden after the games and for Magdalena, Jordan and I to start our holiday. There was just the matter of those two qualifiers to go.

Our preparation was just right, we felt fit and we knew we were at last realising our potential. We beat Slovakia 2–0 with one of our very best performances, full of confidence and bold attacking. It had been a long time since we had played that well and the supporters who packed into that great stadium knew it too. I think if we had kept playing we would simply have kept scoring, we were that dominant.

Of course, it was put in the shade by the Moldova game, which we won 6–0, and I scored four goals, three of them from the penalty spot. We probably didn't play half as well as we had in the previous match, but it didn't matter, as we put a lot of pressure on their defence and kept getting the breaks.

I hadn't scored for Sweden since the 1–1 draw with Turkey back in October, so it was satisfying to get four and silence my critics for a while. A run of a few games without scoring seems like a long barren run when it is at international level, but now all of a sudden I looked like a prolific goalscorer.

It was a good way to finish the season, to say the least. It meant we had overtaken Turkey at the top of Group 4 and, with just three matches remaining, it put us in a great position to qualify. The best thing in football is for your side to be in control of its own destiny. Those results meant that we did not have to rely on other sides making mistakes, we simply had to concentrate on not making any ourselves.

The following morning I sat in the kitchen of the house we have bought in Sweden and read the newspapers, which were pretty complimentary for a change. There was probably an element of relief in the reports as well, in that we were finally looking like a team that could take on some of the best sides in the world. It was a lovely day and I just took it easy with the family. We went for a walk, had a nice lunch and slowly I started to wind down. This was our holiday now and, after all the pressure of the season, we were happy with the way things had turned out. If someone had told me in July that I would be in this position at the end of the season, I would have thought they were mad.

Of course, there is a chance that 2002 could be my last World Cup, so I would love to do well, but we need to ensure we get there first. And there is no such thing as a certainty in football.

chapter thirteen
paradise regained

As I write this, I am sitting in a park in Sweden, watching Jordan play with some other kids a few feet away. The sun is shining and the air is warm. It's a lovely day and I feel completely content. A few weeks ago, I signed an extension to my contract, which will keep me at Celtic for the next three years. So my immediate future is now settled. The roots we have put down in Scotland can continue to grow without the threat of being torn up, and it's great to feel such stability and contentment. Now I'm eager to carry on for Celtic where we left off, at the end of that incredible season.

Celtic's treble season, 2000–2001, was a fantastic experience. It was wonderful to be a part of it all and, now that I'm really able to sit back and put it into perspective, I realise how winning becomes such an addictive habit. I've been taking it easy during the summer, just spending time with my family and letting it all sink in. I'm sure most Celtic fans have been doing the same, enjoying the memory of what we have all achieved together. But I can feel the hunger for more of the same burning inside me.

It was the best season I have ever had since becoming a professional footballer, not just because of all the things we won, but because of the fun and enjoyment I had along the way. I have never played in a team so committed to the cause and so committed to the club and each other. The club spirit has always been good at Celtic, but this season it was better than ever. The knowledge that we were playing to our full potential took away the pressure that stifles creativity and enjoyment. It was replaced with a pressure to maintain a winning standard, and the satisfaction comes from having managed to do just that.

And, once again, it was an honour to play in front of the Celtic fans, who made so many games an experience to remember forever. They were worth countless points to us during the season, home and away, when their support dragged us up from the ground and made us find that extra ounce of effort.

What we achieved was far beyond my expectations. Of course, you go into every season intent on trying to win every competition, but you still know in your mind that the odds are stacked against it. You push yourself and you do your best, but you never expect to defy the odds. There are so many obstacles you have to overcome, so many variables that can go against you. One mistake and you can be out of a cup competition, a run of injuries and your league challenge can fail. To have made a clean sweep of the domestic trophies, and for me to have won the Golden Boot, is just wonderful and it will put this Celtic team in the record books.

Looking back, the start of the season was a key time at Celtic Park. We had a new manager making himself at home in the office, and new players had either arrived or were on the way. We had come off the back of a disappointing season, both for me personally and for the club. My broken leg had robbed me of the chance to play any significant part in the season before and I felt I had a lot to prove. There was everything to play for and a real air of excitement and anticipation. You could tell that the football world was looking at Celtic and wondering what we were going to do. Could we challenge Rangers? Could we reach the required level of commitment and consistency? And we were asking the same questions of ourselves. We knew that Rangers were the team that we had to aim for and the very least we wanted was to close the gap on them.

I'm not sure what I really expected in the lead-up to our first game against Dundee United. I knew I had confidence in the team, that we were capable of great performances and winning things, but players start most seasons with the hope of winning things and most of them end up with nothing. That said, it doesn't mean you should ever start a season without that positive feeling. You should never beat yourself before you have kicked a ball.

I can't give a definitive reason as to why things went so right for us. I was a part of it and I know there is no single answer. Believe me, I've thought about it for long enough. But getting off to a good start was crucial. It meant we never had to play catch-up, never had to change our style, and our confidence was high from day one. Winning does become a habit. It builds confidence and, once players feel confident, they are prepared to try things that they might not try if they're afraid of failure. It's great to know you can give the ball to a teammate who will take defenders on and create openings. I've never enjoyed such a good start to a season and, once that gap started to open up between us and second place, all things seemed to become possible.

That confidence also bred a never-say-die attitude that meant we were winning games even when we didn't play at our best. It's a sign of a good side if they can pull a win out of the bag when the performance may not merit it. There were only a couple of occasions in the whole season when we didn't fight back after going a goal behind. We certainly had a toughness that was lacking the season before.

Football is an unpredictable game and luck plays a major part, but I think you can make your own luck. That's shown in the way that teams that get onto a losing run find it hard to stop the downward spiral, while teams that hit a winning streak seem to get all the breaks. I've mentioned before how there were times when I simply couldn't stop scoring, when I could hit the ball any old way and it would still go in. That was all about being on a roll.

That's the way it is sometimes and you just have to keep riding on the back of that luck, be happy about it and be prepared to battle when it runs out. I can't think of a game when we ever gave up. In every match we played we believed in ourselves. There were times when we played practical football, when we weren't that pretty, but that just showed the character of a team that knew that getting stuck in is every bit as important as playing pretty football.

However, I will always argue that there were plenty of occasions when we played some great football that was both effective and entertaining. Whenever we had the opportunity to stroke the ball around, we did. We just knew when not to take risks.

We did bring in a fair number of new players throughout the season and we were really lucky that they gelled right away, both on the pitch and in the dressing room. Credit for that goes to the management team, who showed a good eye for getting the right kind of players and then made sure they got the best out of them.

Obviously Martin O'Neill had done his homework and the time
he spent watching us play in the pre-season he put to good effect.
He highlighted areas of the team that needed to be strengthened and
brought in the players that he believed could do the job. And you
have to say he got it spot on.

The new guys were tremendous, both as players and as friends.
They were all quality players who were happy to be part of a club
that had ambitions. To be in the Celtic dressing room last season
was an amazing experience. You could feel the confidence exuding
from the players. The guys in that dressing room were desperate to
get out on to the pitch, no matter who the opposition was, just to
show what they could do. Everybody played a part and all those
players who weren't always involved can be proud of the way they
pulled together and contributed to the team effort. Without the
great squad we had, we would not have been half as successful.

Just as our achievement will go down in the record books,
Martin O'Neill will be remembered as the man who turned Celtic
Football Club round in his first season as manager. Together with
John Robertson and Steve Walford, he brought in a training regime
and a club spirit that made the whole season a pleasure. All the
players appreciated the amount we used the ball in match situations
during training, and the fact that we kept battling on right to the
end of the season proved that our fitness did not suffer for the
emphasis on ball work, in fact it probably improved.

On a man-management level Mr O'Neill worked wonders.
There were a number of good players at the club who had been
struggling to find their best form and were low on confidence when
the new management team arrived. Mr O'Neill was able to make

those players realise that they were a valuable part of the club and that they would be given their chance to show what they could do. The slate was wiped clean and it was the start of something new. It was great for those players to know that they were not being judged on anything that had happened before. He made them believe in themselves and motivated the whole team to feel the same.

I would say that, if the management have a magic ingredient, it is communication. They have been brilliant at making it plain what they expect from us. Someone once said, 'Football is a simple game made complicated by idiots.' The last thing that footballers want is to go out on the pitch with a confused idea as to their role. That never happened this season. They kept us on a high from start to finish, never letting us drop off that peak which meant we were focused on every game.

There were a couple of occasions when we didn't get the result we wanted, obviously against Bordeaux and in the second game against Rangers. But those setbacks just served to highlight another side to our character: the determination to bounce back. After we lost to Rangers, there were some amazing articles in the papers, writing us off and suggesting that it was all going to fall apart. Well, we never thought that. A defeat is a defeat, it's not the end of the world, and, as long as you battle back from it, it shouldn't distract you for too long. Just as you don't win the league because of one game, you don't lose it that way either. We always kept that in mind and made sure we never fell into a losing streak.

Of course, there were matches that stand out and there were some that I can now look back on and say probably had a bearing on our season. Obviously, the wins over Rangers were significant and, although it was amazing to beat them 6–2 at Celtic Park, it was possibly more incredible to win 3–0 at Ibrox. But there were other matches, like the 2–1 win over Dundee United in October, or the 1–1 draw with Hibs in February, that earned us valuable points when we could easily have come away with nothing.

There were games I enjoyed because things went right for me, like scoring four in the 6–0 defeat of Kilmarnock in January. But I always feel uncomfortable talking about personal achievements when it's a team game like football. I genuinely believe that anything that I have done has only been possible because of the quality of the players that I have had around me. They have given me the ball when I have been in good positions and they have played with a sense of purpose that has meant we are always a threat. Right through the team, from the keeper to my fellow strikers, there have been huge performances all season.

But I am very proud that I have scored so many goals that have helped Celtic win things, and it has been incredibly satisfying for me to have done the job that I am paid to do. I've scored 53 goals, 35 of them in the league, and that is the most I have ever scored in one season as a professional. It will be in the Celtic record books, and to leave a mark like that is brilliant. Some have been well-taken efforts that I've looked back at and thought 'not bad'. Others have been less memorable. But, as they say, they all count and you have to be there in order to score in the first place.

I was sitting watching TV at our house in Sweden when I got a call to say that I had won the Golden Boot. After all that we had won as a team, this was just the icing on the cake for me. It will be one of those things that I'll be able to look back on in years to come and use to impress the grandchildren. I'm not a great hoarder of memorabilia, but that will certainly have a place somewhere among my most cherished possessions.

To add to the personal accolades, I was also named Players' Player of the Year and Football Writers' Player of the Year. It makes you feel quite humble to have those who watched you play all season decide you're the best player they've seen. Last season, when I was working to regain my fitness after breaking my leg, I didn't know what level I could get back to. Now I do, and I feel fitter than ever.

Like any award winner, I have to hand it to the guys around me, without whom I wouldn't be the one in the limelight. They have given me the opportunity to score so many goals. Because UEFA give SPL players fewer points per goal then strikers in England, Spain or Italy, it meant that to win the Golden Boot I had to score a lot. But believe me, the SPL isn't an easy league to score in. Defences are very strong and you have to work as a team to create every opportunity. I've been lucky to have had some brilliant players partnering me up front, particularly Chris Sutton and Alan Thompson.

If our march to the treble looked like a steady procession from start to finish, emotionally the season was full of ups and downs. We spent a large part of it under the shadow of the illnesses of Alan Stubbs and Morten Wieghorst. But things like that draw the team together even more. It has been tough for everybody, especially the families of those guys, and to watch them slowly getting better has been a joy and a relief. The news of their illnesses shook the whole club, and we found it quite difficult to get any happiness out of the games we were winning until we felt sure that they were going to be okay. It was a wonderful moment to see Stubbsie come on and score in the 5–2 win over Hibs in May. That will probably be one of the best memories of a season that is packed with them.

Morten and Stubbsie are now doing well, and it's great to have them back playing football again, and I wish Stubbsie all the best at Everton. Didier Agathe is another who will now have to wait to get back into the thick of things following his leg break. But he's a strong and determined guy and I'm sure he will make it back as good as ever.

It's strange when you contrast those sad or tragic moments with the highs of winning trophies. I suppose the game that will stick in my memory for the longest is the day we beat St Mirren 1–0 to finally clinch the SPL title. It was 7 April, obviously a great date, as I've said for a long time that seven is a lucky number.

There had been so much pressure over those weeks leading up to the game, with so many people seeming to think that the title was already in the bag. We knew it wasn't and that, if we let our guard slip for a moment and didn't remain 100 per cent focused, we could end up throwing it all away. We knew it was just around the corner, but to finally secure it after all those months felt great. When it came to the crunch, both in the league and in the cup competitions, we played well.

I may be sitting here in the sun in Sweden, but it is easy to let my mind drift back to those days, winning the league, picking up the cups at Hampden Park. If I close my eyes, I can see the crowd cheering and waving their scarves and flags. I can hear the roar. I also remember the look on Magdalena's face, how happy and proud she was. I have the medals to prove what happened, but for me I also have the memories that I hope will never fade.

People have asked me about my favourite games and favourite goals and that's tough, because so many are significant. I think my favourite game must be the one that clinched the SPL title, but the third goal in the CIS Final has to be my favourite goal. You always dream of scoring in cup finals, and to get one like that is an amazing feeling. I've actually only seen it once on video since the game, but I'm sure it will get a few more airings over the coming months. Because I was so tired at the time and things seemed to happen in slow motion, I remember almost everything about it. It's probably one of the best goals I have ever scored.

Looking forward, which I do with confidence, I know that it is up to every one of us at the club to prove that what we did last season was not a one-off, a freak. Having done it once, we all believe we can do it again and it is all in our own hands. When you have had a season like 2000–2001, you become aware of how great it is to win. It is an emotion that I want to experience as often as possible before I finally hang up my boot,s and it's the emotion I want to feel wearing the green and white hoops of Celtic.

Of course, it will be even more difficult in the season to come, because every team now knows us and what we are capable of. They know our players and the way we approach the game. Perhaps we won't be quite the surprise that we were last year. And being champions and cup winners, oh, and CIS cup winners, means that we are the top scalp, the one that everyone wants more than any other. Celtic are always a target, but now we are right at the top of the tree for everyone to shoot at. There isn't a team in Scotland that doesn't want to knock us off our perch.

The threats in the SPL, like Rangers, Hibs, Hearts and Dundee

United, will be plotting our downfall, and you can bet that every small side will be praying to draw us in a cup competition. We are well aware that every game is going to be a cup final for the next year at least. The tension will be unbelievable, but I am convinced that we have the maturity to cope. We also have some great young players waiting in the wings for their chance to make an impression on the big stages. And I'm sure all of us are happier being the team at the top than being one of the ones trying to get there. Staying the best is the sort of pressure we want.

I'm really glad that I now know I will be a part of Celtic's campaign for the next few years, having got my contract discussions tied up. It can be a bit unsettling for everyone when things like that drag on, but it is important to get the right agreement. Fortunately, all parties essentially wanted the same thing, so we were all moving in the same direction. I never wanted to leave Celtic and I was very happy that we got it all sorted. I was always confident that we would.

My family are very happy in Scotland, we love the way of life here, the people, the country, and we feel totally at home in Bothwell. We have been shown nothing but kindness, and made a lot of really good friends. I believe that Celtic Football Club offers me the chance to achieve the things that I want to achieve in football. I've never been one to predict the future, but I'm confident that we can compete for everything and that includes Europe. It would be great to make an impression in the Champions League and that's something we will have to concentrate on, I'm sure.

It will be up to the manager to decide whether we need to bring in new players to support our challenge and I'm sure he will work hard to get exactly the right balance. It is always good to expand a squad, to cover for players who might get injured and to give more options. You only have to look around at other top sides to see the sort of squads they have built up. When we played Manchester United in Tommy Boyd's testimonial game, they could have fielded two teams and the second would have given most sides a good run for their money.

The only way we can really improve on last season is to get a good run in Europe, but we'll just have to see what happens. All the players are hungry for even more success and we will give it everything we've got, but playing in Europe is a learning process and we will have to be patient.

It has been an amazing experience ever since I joined Celtic, and this season has been the icing on that particular cake. Ask any footballer if he wants to play for a club where 60,000 fervent fans turn up nearly every week and he'll jump at the opportunity. I really feel a part of this great club, its history and traditions, its big family of fans, both in Scotland and all over the world.

Celtic came along at a time when I was at a very low point in my career and I needed to get away from a situation that could have destroyed me as a player. The move to Glasgow gave me the chance to start again, to rebuild my career at a club that had belief in me and was prepared to let me play football in the way I wanted and knew was best for me and the team. That has never changed. Celtic has remained a great place to play football and I feel proud to say it is my club.

celtic results

SATURDAY 26 MAY
Tennents Scottish FA Cup (Final)
Celtic 3 **Hibernian** 0 FT
McNamara 39, Larsson 48, pen 80
Half-time: 1–0

SUNDAY 20 MAY
Scottish Premier
Kilmarnock 1 **Celtic** 0 FT
Mahood 78
Attend: 12,675 Half-time: 0–0

SUNDAY 13 MAY
Scottish Premier
Celtic 0 **Dundee** 2 FT
Caballero 29, 42
Attend: 59,435 Half-time: 0–2

SUNDAY 6 MAY
Scottish Premier
Hibernian 2 **Celtic** 5 FT
Libbra 85, 88, McNamara 5, 18,
Larsson 62, Stubbs 68, Moravcik 80
Attend: 8,728 Half-time: 0–2

SUNDAY 29 APRIL
Scottish Premier
Rangers 0 **Celtic** 3 FT
Moravcik 61, 74, Larsson 87
Attend: 50,057 Half-time: 0–0

SUNDAY 22 APRIL
Scottish Premier
Celtic 1 **Hearts** 0 FT
Moravcik 68
Attend: 59,298 Half-time: 0–0

SUNDAY 15 APRIL
Tennents Scottish FA Cup (Semi Final)

Celtic 3 **Dundee Utd** 1 FT
Larsson 32, pen 79, McNamara 80,
Lilley 84
Attend: 38,699 Half-time: 1–0

SATURDAY 7 APRIL
Scottish Premier
Celtic 1 **St Mirren** 0 FT
Johnson 38
Attend: 60,440 Half-time: 1–0

WEDNESDAY 4 APRIL
Scottish Premier
Celtic 2 **Dundee** 1 FT
Johnson 5, Mjallby 84, Sara 67
Attend: 59,562 Half-time: 1–0

SUNDAY 1 APRIL
Scottish Premier
Aberdeen 0 **Celtic** 1 FT
Agathe 73
Attend: 16,067 Half-time: 0–0

SUNDAY 18 MARCH
CIS Insurance Cup (Final)
Celtic 3 **Kilmarnock** 0 FT
Larsson 47, 74, 81
Attend: 48,830 Half-time: 0–0

WEDNESDAY 14 MARCH
Scottish Premier
St Johnstone 1 **Celtic** 2 FT
McCluskey 41, Johnson 28, Larsson 61
Attend: 8,993 Half-time: 1–1

SUNDAY 11 MARCH
Tennents Scottish FA Cup
(Quarter Final)
Celtic 1 **Hearts** 0 FT

Larsson 40
Attend: 34,672 Half-time: 1–0

WEDNESDAY 7 MARCH
Tennents Scottish FA Cup
(Fourth Round replay)
Celtic 4 Dunfermline 1 FT
Vega 23, 48, Larsson pen 61, pen 73
Thomson 28
Attend: 31,940 Half-time: 1–1

SUNDAY 4 MARCH
Scottish Premier
Dunfermline 0 Celtic 3 FT
Petrov 11, Larsson 25, Lennon 77
Attend: 9,096 Half-time: 0–2

SUNDAY 25 FEBRUARY
Scottish Premier
Celtic 1 Hibernian 1 FT
Mjallby 23, Libbra 84
Attend: 60,063 Half-time: 1–0

WEDNESDAY 21 FEBRUARY
Scottish Premier
Celtic 1 Motherwell 0 FT
Moravcik 83
Attend: 58,880 Half-time: 0–0

SATURDAY 17 FEBRUARY
Tennents Scottish FA Cup
(Fourth Round)
Dunfermline 2 Celtic 2 FT
Skerla 83, Nicholson 90, Larsson 66, 88
Attend: 11,222 Half-time: 0–0

SUNDAY 11 FEBRUARY
Scottish Premier
Celtic 1 Rangers 0 FT
Thompson 17,
Attend: 59,496 Half-time: 1–0

WEDNESDAY 7 FEBRUARY
CIS Insurance Cup (Semi Final)
Celtic 3 Rangers 1 FT
Sutton 6, Larsson 17, pen 69, Albertz

pen 37
Attend: 50,000 Half-time: 2–1

SUNDAY 4 FEBRUARY
Scottish Premier
Hearts 0 Celtic 3 FT
Larsson 4, 68, 83
Attend: 13,077 Half-time: 0–1

SUNDAY 28 JANUARY
Tennents Scottish FA Cup (Third Round)
Stranraer 1 Celtic 4 FT
Harty 84, Valgaeren 23, McNamara 51,
Knox og 55, Moravcik 85
Attend: 5,600 Half-time: 0–1

TUESDAY 2 JANUARY
Scottish Premier
Celtic 6 Kilmarnock 0 FT
Sutton 37, 61, Larsson 53, 69, 72, 86
Attend: 59,380 Half-time: 1–0

TUESDAY 26 DECEMBER
Scottish Premier
Dundee Utd 0 Celtic 4 FT
Larsson pen 22, Sutton 33, 40, Petrov 72
Attend: 12,306 Half-time: 0–3

SATURDAY 23 DECEMBER
Scottish Premier
St Mirren 0 Celtic 2 FT
Agathe 13, Larsson 62
Attend: 9,487 Half-time: 0–1

SATURDAY 16 DECEMBER
Scottish Premier
Celtic 6 Aberdeen 0 FT
Larsson 4, 76, 78, Vega 17, 81, Smith 89
Attend: 60,013 Half-time: 2–0

SUNDAY 10 DECEMBER
Scottish Premier
Dundee 1 Celtic 2 FT
Boyd og 55, Petrov 4, Agathe 90
Attend: 10,763 Half-time: 0–1

SATURDAY 2 DECEMBER
Scottish Premier
Celtic 3 Dunfermline 1 FT
Moravcik 7, Larsson 20, Johnson 80,
Dair 1
Attend: 59,244 Half-time: 2–1

WEDNESDAY 29 NOVEMBER
Scottish Premier
Hibernian 0 Celtic 0 FT
Attend: 14,939 Half-time: 0–0

SUNDAY 26 NOVEMBER
Scottish Premier
Rangers 5 Celtic 1 FT
Ferguson 34, Flo 60, de Boer 68,
Amoruso 76, Mols 85, Larsson 56
Attend: 50,083 Half-time: 1–0

SATURDAY 18 NOVEMBER
Scottish Premier
Celtic 6 Hearts 1 FT
Valgaeren 15, Moravcik 36, Larsson 39,
81, Mjallby 44, Petrov 82, Cameron 13
Attend: 59,813 Half-time: 4–1

SUNDAY 12 NOVEMBER
Scottish Premier
Celtic 4 St Johnstone 1 FT
Sutton 12, Larsson 34, 59, Moravcik 37,
Russell 82
Attend: 57,137 Half-time: 3–0

THURSDAY 9 NOVEMBER
UEFA Cup (Second Round, 2nd Leg)
Celtic 1 Bordeaux 2 AET
Moravcik 54, Laslandes 78, 114
Attend: 51,242 Half-time: 0–0
(1–1 after 90 mins)
Bordeaux won 3–2 on aggregate

SUNDAY 5 NOVEMBER
Scottish Premier
Kilmarnock 0 Celtic 1 FT
Thompson 60
Attend: 13,417 Half-time: 0–0

WEDNESDAY 1 NOVEMBER
CIS Insurance Cup (Quarter Final)
Hearts 2 Celtic 5 AET
Cameron pen 36, pen 70, Crainey 41,
Smith 60, Healy 99, Moravcik 116,
McNamara 117
Attend: 13,076 Half-time: 1–1
(2–2 after 90 mins)

SUNDAY 29 OCTOBER
Scottish Premier
Motherwell 3 Celtic 3 FT
Adams 22, McCulloch 53, Brannan pen
78, Mjallby 13, Valgaeren 57,
McNamara 71
Attend: 10,820 Half-time: 1–1

THURSDAY 26 OCTOBER
UEFA Cup (Second Round, 1st Leg)
Bordeaux 1 Celtic 1 FT
Dugarry 23, Larsson pen 25
Attend: 21,318 Half-time: 1–1

SATURDAY 21 OCTOBER
Scottish Premier
Celtic 2 Dundee Utd 1 FT
Larsson 34, Thompson 62,
Lambert og 78
Attend: 59,427 Half-time: 1–0

TUESDAY 17 OCTOBER
Scottish Premier
St Johnstone 0 Celtic 2 FT
Valgaeren 42, Larsson pen 86,
Attend: 8,946 Half-time: 0–1

SATURDAY 14 OCTOBER
Scottish Premier
Celtic 2 St Mirren 0 FT
Sutton 33, Larsson 85
Attend: 60,002 Half-time: 1–0

SUNDAY 1 OCTOBER
Scottish Premier
Aberdeen 1 Celtic 1 FT
Winters 45, Larsson 82

Attend: 18,239 Half-time: 1–0

THURSDAY 28 SEPTEMBER
UEFA Cup (First Round, 2nd Leg)
HJK Helsinki 2 Celtic 1 AET
Roiha 41, 75, Sutton 117
Attend: 6,530 Half-time: 1–0
(2-0 after 90 mins)
Celtic won 3–2 on aggregate

SATURDAY 23 SEPTEMBER
Scottish Premier
Celtic 1 Dundee 0 FT
Petrov 61
Attend: 59,694 Half-time: 0–0

MONDAY 18 SEPTEMBER
Scottish Premier
Dunfermline 1 Celtic 2 FT
Crawford pen 60, Larsson pen 62, 85
Attend: 9,493 Half-time: 0–0

THURSDAY 14 SEPTEMBER
UEFA Cup (First Round, 1st Leg)
Celtic 2 HJK Helsinki 0 FT
Larsson 14, 25,
Attend: 40,544 Half-time: 2–0

SATURDAY 9 SEPTEMBER
Scottish Premier
Celtic 3 Hibernian 0 FT
Larsson pen 16, 45, Burchill 90
Attend: 60,091 Half-time: 2–0

TUESDAY 5 SEPTEMBER
CIS Insurance Cup (Third Round)
Celtic 4 Raith 0 FT
Sutton 41, Johnson pen 44, 55,
Thompson 68
Attend: 32,307 Half-time: 2–0

SUNDAY 27 AUGUST
Scottish Premier
Celtic 6 Rangers 2 FT
Sutton 1, 90, Petrov 8, Lambert 11,
Larsson 50, 62, Reyna 40, Dodds pen 55

Attend: 59,476 Half-time: 3–1

THURSDAY 24 AUGUST
UEFA Cup
(First Qualifying Round 2nd Leg)
Celtic 7 Jeunesse Esch 0 FT
Burchill 12, 14, 15, Berkovic 2, 46,
Riseth 52, Petrov 71,
Attend: 40,282 Half-time: 4–0

SATURDAY 19 AUGUST
Scottish Premier
Hearts 2 Celtic 4 FT
Severin 56, Juanjo 65, Sutton 22, 26,
Larsson 39, Moravcik 62,
Attend: 16,744   Half-time: 0–3

SUNDAY 13 AUGUST
Scottish Premier
Celtic 2 Kilmarnock 1 FT
Larsson 50, Johnson 72, McLaren 17
Attend: 58,054 Half-time: 0–1

THURSDAY 10 AUGUST
UEFA Cup
(First Qualifying Round, 1st Leg)
Jeunesse Esch 0 Celtic 4 FT
Moravcik 37, 58, Larsson 61, Petta 81
Attend: 4,004 Half-time: 0–1

SATURDAY 5 AUGUST
Scottish Premier
Celtic 1 Motherwell 0 FT
Petrov 11
Attend: 58,534 Half-time: 1–0

SUNDAY 30 JULY
Scottish Premier
Dundee Utd 1 Celtic 2 FT
McCracken 49, Larsson 37, Sutton 66
Attend: 11,761 Half-time: 0–1

index

Aberdeen 98, 105-7 *passim*, 148
Agathe, Didier 95-6, 104, 116, 119, 122, 123, 154, 181
Ajax 71, 102
Anderson, Kennet 15
Andersson, Patrik 44, 45, 163
Ardiles, Ossie 138, 162
awards 27, 115, 174, 179-80 *see also individual entries*
Azerbaijan 162-5 *passim*

basketball 116-17
Belgium 43-4
Berkovic, Eyal 60, 66, 125
Blinker, Reggie 34, 54
Bordeaux 51
   Girondins de 90-3, 103, 178
Bosnich, Mark 62, 68
Boyd, Tom 48, 83-4, 126, 184
Brazil 15, 118, 119
van Bronckhorst, Giovanni 75
Bulgaria 15, 119
Burchill, Mark 60, 66, 86, 96

Cameroon 15, 117-18
di Canio, Paulo 52
Celtic FC 19-21, 25-8, 37-40, 46-57, 61-159, 165, 173-84
   and Europe 27, 61-2, 64-5, 87-94, 184
   fans 26, 35, 51, 53-6 *passim*, 61, 73, 76-7, 81, 84, 86, 90, 100, 106, 108, 119, 120, 126, 135-8 *passim* 141, 144, 156-8 *passim*, 166, 174; American 114-15
   history 83-4

and Rangers 71-81, 125-8
   training 37, 46, 49-50, 89, 110, 114, 134, 137, 157, 177
Champions League 87, 183
CIS Cup 84-5, 104, 125-7, 130, 131, 133-45, 147, 182
Clark, John (kit man) 115, 150
Combe, Alan 55
Crainey, Stephen 104, 112, 113, 138, 139

Dahline, Martin 118
Dalglish, Kenny 39-40, 46, 138, 162
Dodds, Billy 80
Dugarry, Christophe 90
Dundee 86, 95, 97-8, 106, 148, 149, 151
Dundee United 39-40, 47, 53-6, 61, 102, 105, 106, 147, 148, 175, 179, 182
Dunfermline 106, 107, 129, 147

English Premier League 102
European Cup/Championship 15, 20, 38, 43-5, 49, 50, 163
European league 61-2

Ferguson, Barry 75, 80, 81
Feyenoord FC, Rotterdam 10-11, 14-23, 37, 60, 71, 102, 110, 159
Finland 161
Florida 110-17, 119
Fotheringham, Mark 53
Francis, Trevor 50

Gleneagles 112
Golden Boot award 174, 179, 181

golf 13, 31, 38-9, 60, 111-12
Grasshoppers, Zurich 14, 20
Gould, Jonathan 78, 79

van Hanegem, Wim (Feyenoord coach) 16, 21, 22
Havutcu, Tayfur 167
Healy, Colin 66, 106, 112, 113, 137, 139
Hearts 37, 67-9 *passim*, 104, 105, 122-5, 147, 182
Helsingborgs IF 11, 13, 14, 19, 66, 116
Helsinki 87-8
Hibernian (Hibs) 26, 85-6, 105, 106, 110, 125, 129, 130, 148-9, 154-6, 179, 182
Hogaborg BK 12, 14, 66
Howley, John (president, Orlando Celtic Supporters' Club) 115

Inverness Caledonian Thistle 65, 121
Italy 45, 98

Jansen, Rob (agent) 19-20, 22
Jansen, Wim (coach) 14, 15-16, 20, 23
Jeunesse Esch 61, 64-7, 125
Johnson, Tommy 52, 73, 103, 107, 119, 148
Johnstone, Jimmy 150
Jordan, Michael 32, 117

Kanoute, Frederic 52
Kilmarnock 67, 104, 106-8 *passim*, 130, 131, 139-43, 149-51 *passim*, 179
Klos, Stefan 78, 126
Konterman 75, 79

Lagerback, Lars (Swedish coach) 40, 43, 44
Lambert, Paul 63, 68, 77, 86, 104, 114, 124-5, 131, 137
Larsson, Hendrik
  arrival in Scotland 9-11, 23
  awards 27, 115, 174, 197-80
  breaking leg 27-31, 174; recovery 35-41
  character 14, 70, 133-4
  childhood/adolescence 12-13, 16, 66, 89, 124, 137-8, 161-2
  and Feyenoord 10-11, 14-23, 37, 60, 96, 110, 159

hair 99-100
  injuries 150-1, 165
  pre-match preparation 54-5, 74-7, 134-6, 152-3
  scoring goals 14, 89; for Celtic 26, 27, 37, 55, 68-9, 79-80, 86, 87, 91-2, 98-9, 105, 107, 108, 120, 123-4, 126, 127, 129, 130, 140-2 *passim*, 149, 155-6, 179, 181-2; for Sweden 15, 19, 45, 118, 119, 161, 167, 171
  training 40, 49-50, 123
Larsson, Jordan (son) 30-2, 57, 68, 96-7, 109, 110, 117, 120, 158, 173
Larsson, Kim and Robert (brothers) 161
Larsson, Magdalena (wife) 14, 17, 20, 23, 29-35 *passim*, 38, 51-2, 57, 68, 69, 99, 110, 181
Laslandes, Lillian 93
Lennon, Neil 62, 104-5, 124-5, 139
Libbra, Mark 129, 148, 154
Lisbon Lions 115, 150
Ljunberg, Fredrik 163
Lynch, Simon 66

Macedonia 162, 169
Mahe, Stephane 56, 81
Malcom, Robert 126
Malmo 50
Maloney, Shaun 113
Malta 168-9
Manchester United 102, 184
Marshall, Gordon 139
McDermott, Terry 138, 162
McGeown, Mark 122
McLeish, Alex (Hibernian manager) 85
McNamara, Jackie 55, 63, 86, 104, 120, 122, 154, 155
Milan 83
Mjallby, Johan 44, 45, 63, 74, 80, 97, 103, 104, 115, 126, 129, 163
Moldova 162, 169-71
Mols, Michael 127
Moravcik, Lubo 63, 68, 69, 77, 78, 84-7 *passim*, 91, 93, 97, 104, 108, 122, 127, 139, 140, 141, 151, 154
Motherwell 61-3, 103-4, 129
Murdoch, Bobby 149-50

Nilsson, Roland 163
Norwich City 119-20

Old Firm matches 26, 70-81, 106
Olympique 26-8 *passim*
O'Neil, John 154
O'Neill, Martin 46-7, 49-51, 53, 56, 60, 62, 64,
    67-70, 79, 81, 94, 95, 115, 120, 127, 135-7
    passim, 144, 148, 153, 157, 174, 177-8
Overmars, Marc 95

Paatelainen, Mixu 148
Pele 138
penalties, scoring from 15, 86, 91-2, 118, 156,
    171
Person, Bent (Hogaborg coach) 12-13, 19
Petrov, Stilian 52, 63, 77, 93, 98, 108, 130-1,
    144-5
Petta, Bobby 51, 52, 66-8 *passim*, 77, 78, 80, 91,
    98, 115, 120, 129, 131, 137, 138, 151, 153
Petterson, Jorgen 43
del Piero, Alessandro 45
Player of Year, Football Writers' 27, 180
    Players' 27, 180
PSV 102

Raith Rovers 84-5
Rangers 26, 35, 71-81, 102, 105-6, 125-8, 130,
    131, 148, 149, 151, 156, 158, 165, 175,
    178-9, 182
Real Madrid 102
Real Zarogaza 15
Reyna, Claudio 78, 117, 127
Rieper, Marc 31, 34, 37-9 *passim*, 59-60
Robertson, John 50, 144, 177
Romania 15, 118
Ruddock, Neil 52
Russia 118

Saudi Arabia 118
Sauzee, Franck 148
Scott, Brian (physio) 35, 36, 41, 119
Scottish Cup 27, 121-2, 129, 130, 147, 152-6,
    170
Scottish Premier League 26, 72, 97-8, 102-3, 105,
    122, 125, 128, 147, 149, 180, 181
Shearer, Alan 48

Sheppard, Tim (Norwich physio) 119
Slovakia 162, 168, 170, 171
Smith, Jamie 'Smudger' 104, 112, 113
Soderberg, Tommy (Swedish coach) 168
Souness, Graham 138
Spain 98, 102
St Johnstone 26, 37, 102, 105, 130, 133
St Mirren 102, 106, 109, 147, 148, 168, 181
Stranraer 114, 121-2
Stubbs, Alan 59, 77, 100-2 *passim*, 114, 115,
    131, 180-1
Sutton, Chris 47-8, 55-7 *passim*, 63, 65, 68, 73,
    75-7 *passim*, 79, 81, 87, 88, 90, 103, 104,
    108, 110, 126, 128, 129, 131-2, 137, 139,
    140, 143-4, 151, 155, 156, 180
Svensson, Anders 163, 165, 169
Sweden, playing for 15, 38, 40-1, 43-5, 117-19,
    161-72
Swedish Premier League 14
Switzerland 170

Tampa Bay Mutiny 117, 119
Thompson, Alan 48, 86, 95, 97-8, 103, 108,
    110, 115, 116, 123, 128, 130, 180
Trustfull, Orlando 14
Tugay, 79, 162
Turkey 44, 162-3, 166-7, 171

UEFA Cup 26-8, 38, 61, 64-7 *passim*, 87-94
University of South Florida 115-16

Valderrama, Carlos 119
Valgaeren, Joos 43, 47, 73, 77, 84-6 *passim*, 97,
    122, 124, 131
Vega, Ramon 107, 122, 124, 126, 140

Walford, Steve 177
Wallace, Rod 80
Walsh, Steve (coach) 49, 50
West Ham 52-3
Wieghorst, Morten 101-2, 114, 115, 131, 180-1
Wilfrid, Brother 83
Winters, Robbie 98
World Cup 15, 19, 158, 162-72
    in US 15, 117-19, 162

picture credits